The Third Journey

The Third Journey
Making the Most of Your Life after Work

OLDERHOOD.COM FOUNDERS
William R. Storie and Robin W. Trimingham

THE THIRD JOURNEY
MAKING THE MOST OF YOUR LIFE AFTER WORK

iUniverse books may be ordered through booksellers or by contacting:

iUniverse
1663 Liberty Drive
Bloomington, IN 47403
www.iuniverse.com
1-800-Authors (1-800-288-4677)

ISBN: 978-1-5320-1328-7 (sc)
ISBN: 978-1-5320-1329-4 (hc)
ISBN: 978-1-5320-1327-0 (e)

Library of Congress Control Number: 2017901723

Print information available on the last page.

iUniverse rev. date: 04/05/2017

For everyone

CONTENTS

Health Considerations

Estate Planning

Quality of Life

Money Matters

Ready, Steady, Go

FOREWORD

Bill Storie and Robin Trimingham have done something quite unique. They have written a book about retirement that is practical, engaging, at times funny, and hard to put down. The critical issues of financial and physical health, relationships, the effect of change, legal concerns, and discovering the passions and pursuits that fill one's time productively are dealt with in a way that sets *The Third Journey* apart.

Most of us are both excited and a bit afraid of what may happen during Olderhood, the name the authors give this exciting and challenging stage of life. Blending facts, possibilities, options, and true life stories to make a point come alive, this is the guide you need to help you enter this phase of life with confidence.

Bill and Robin have built an Internet presence that has followers in all corners of the globe through Olderhood.com's website and Facebook presence. They added a way for retirees to exchange ideas and concerns with each other through a growing network of virtual and in-person clubs.

Now, *The Third Journey* brings all of their collective experience and solid advice to your home. It is truly a road map to your future.

Bob Lowry
Author of *Living a Satisfying Retirement* and *Building a Satisfying Retirement*

PREFACE

Once upon a time in the far-off land of Bermuda, a bank manager named Bill was discussing his impending retirement with a friend. He confessed that while he had all his financial ducks in a row, he was hesitant to accept a lucrative early retirement package because he had no idea what he was going to do with all his free time. He knew that he wanted to set up an office and continue consulting and also pursue his passion to write, but he was not sure if this would be sufficient to fill his day.

To forestall having to commit himself to anything in particular, he busied himself with renting office space downtown, finding suitable furnishings, and setting up shop.

For a brief while he zipped from one pasta-and-cappuccino lunch to the next, exploring the possibilities. He quickly realized that a spate of mundane business analysis would never satisfy his newly liberated psyche, for his soul was craving an adventure—a wild foray into uncharted waters.

As he cast about for some way to satisfy this yearning, he suddenly had an idea—he would create a blog and write about his struggles to transition from the work world to something more fulfilling. In a moment of recklessness, he mentioned this to his longtime business colleague, Robin, who replied, "Brilliant idea! There's just one tiny problem, isn't there? You don't actually know how to start a blog, do you?"

"No idea."

"Not a problem; I do. So what are we going to call it?"

This required quite a bit of thought because the hardest part of naming something these days is not coming up with a name but coming up with a name that is still available for purchase as a dot-com. Many brilliant possibilities surfaced, but regrettably they were already claimed by someone else. For the better part of a week, the working title was actually *Gentleman Geezers*, simply because it was available. Thankfully, common sense prevailed on the basis that neither one of the authors is a "geezer," nor was the phrase likely to attract many female readers.

In fact, the more we thought about it, the more we realized that there just did not seem to be a suitable word for what we wanted to write about. The more we considered the meaning of words like senior, golden-ager, elder, and retiree, the more we realized that all these words had been assigned negative connotations of infirmity, frailty, and diminished mental capacity. This, we agreed, was *not* what we wanted to write about at all.

The more we hunted through the thesaurus, the more we realized that what we wanted was a word that did not exist—a word that conveyed life and energy and opportunity and vitality as it pertained to an older person. And then it dawned on us—if we wanted to discuss an entirely new kind of life for "postretirement adulthood," we were going to have to start by defining exactly what this life entailed and then create a vocabulary to describe it. That was a watershed moment for us that changed the course of the entire project.

"The tricky thing is that all the good words are taken," said Robin.

"They can't be," said Bill.

"They are."

"Then where does that leave us?"

"Trying to come up with a new word for 'old,' I think."

"Hell no—*I'm not old! I'm just older!*" said Bill emphatically.

After weighing the merits of just about every word combination we could think of, we eventually named the blog "Olderhood," our idea being that one transitions from childhood (your first life journey), through adulthood (your second life journey) to eventually arrive at a postretirement phase of life, which we termed Olderhood.

The "Third Journey," therefore, is your passage through this third phase of life.

Before we embarked on this project, we would have said that retirement life was a time of creaky knees, conserving resources, and mending fences. We also *assumed* that although there were retired people all over the world, retirement concerns would vary greatly, depending upon ethnic, social, cultural, financial, and geographic considerations. We embarked on this project as a hobby, and we did *hope* that some people would be interested in what we had to say, but we never really thought that our voice would reach beyond North America.

Much to our amazement, we were completely wrong.

We launched www.olderhood.com in May 2013 and quickly discovered that retirement concerns cut horizontally through all levels of society in every country in the world. Everyone is concerned about health, finances, aging, keeping busy, maintaining their independence, and how to make a productive contribution to society.

In August of that year we also started a Facebook page (www.facebook. com/Olderhoodcom) as a companion to the blog and immediately found that people in locations around the world were desperate for lighthearted but accurate information on these six common concerns and a safe forum in which to share their experiences and seek advice. In less than six months we had followers from the United States, Canada, the United Kingdom, France, Australia, New Zealand, India, the Philippines, and Malaysia.

The multicultural appeal that two people from Bermuda, a tiny country in the second most isolated community on the planet, had achieved was both astonishing and humbling. On New Year's Day 2014, we celebrated the addition of our fifteen thousandth Facebook fan,[1] as we endeavored to comprehend that perhaps we had found our mission—a mission so simple and yet so vast it would take the rest of our lives to

---

1. At the time of this writing, we have over seventy-five thousand followers and continue to grow daily.

fulfill: to *create a road map for a new postretirement lifestyle that anyone can follow*.

As daunting and impossible as this initially seemed, it was equally clear that we would have no shortage of help because our readers were not shy about telling us what they liked and wanted, and they enthusiastically encouraged their friends and family to write to us as well. Most surprising of all was that these people were willing to stand up and share their thoughts and feelings and emotions publicly online.

Given the diverse time zones in which our Facebook followers reside, we soon discovered that we were actually operating a twenty-four-hour "business." It might have been three o'clock in the morning on our island, but it was three in the afternoon in central Manila, and every member of our expanding Philippine community wanted to chat with us and with each other.

To accommodate the nonstop activity, we decided to open a special group so that our most active members in Asia and India would have a place to convene and entertain each other while we got a little sleep. Although we were not certain whether anyone would like this idea, we named this Facebook group the Olderhood International Club (OIC) and ran a couple of notices on our main Facebook page to let people know how they could join. Our first member, a resident of Malaysia, joined in less than four minutes and promptly signed up all of his friends and relatives. Within a month there were well over one hundred regulars chatting and sharing information around the clock, and the more we listened to them and interacted with them, the more we learned.

A great number of our new friends proved to be highly educated retired professionals who are interested in natural remedies, sharing recipes, humor, wisdom, and battling loneliness and are willing to help each other with everything from advice regarding how to fill out pension forms to praying for the recovery of a loved one. Far from whining about failing health and sorry circumstances all day long, these people help each other up when they are down and have a huge appetite for friendship, fellowship, and humor.

They are also anything but shy, and they have offered their opinions, their perspectives, and their hearts to us on every step of this journey; many of the ideas that we have developed in this book were germinated as a result of our interactions with them. They have enthusiastically "liked" the material that resonated with them and kept politely silent on things that did not. They helped us cut a new path for everyone to follow. We gratefully acknowledge these wonderful people from all corners of the globe and recognize their support.

In our efforts to develop original, quality content for our online audience, we tested most of our potential material on the OIC group. They heard our first podcast, watched our first video blog, completed surveys, and downloaded e-books. They offered comments on hundreds of original inspirational quotes, phrases, and terms, some of which you will find in this book.

We were just starting to get the hang of all this when something completely unanticipated happened—our Philippine OIC members suddenly decided that they wanted to form a proper club and hold face-to-face gatherings. Today, there are several OIC clubs in the Philippines that meet regularly and even go on group vacations. (See Appendix A for information on starting a local chapter of the Olderhood International Club in your area.)

Obviously, we now had no shortage of data regarding the interests, needs, and preferences of English-speaking people over the age of fifty. The more we analyzed the trends buried among our most popular posts, the more we began to realize that this third phase of life is not actually about retirement at all.

The third phase of life is about challenging traditional boundaries, conquering old fears, staying positive, and finding a meaningful purpose to carry you through the rest of your life.

At first we didn't realize that we had actually identified a universal gap in human understanding, but the further we went, the more it became obvious that we were compiling information that everyone seemed to need. As we struggled to maintain control of this ever-expanding project, it eventually became clear that we should write a book, and the idea for *The Third Journey* was born.

The objective of *The Third Journey* is to help you develop and maintain a thriving new lifestyle, once the work years are behind you. It is a compilation of the thoughts and life experiences of both the authors, combined with research from a wide variety of accredited sources and insights contributed from many of our blog readers. It explores the origins of retirement, popular misconceptions about growing older, and the traditional impacts of the aging process, and it offers some new ideas for the third phase of your life.

We hope this book becomes the guidebook that you refer to time and again as your retirement life progresses.

ACKNOWLEDGMENTS

The authors would like to acknowledge Bob Lowry and Dr. Bob Ritzema for their support and encouragement during the writing of this book and the members of the Olderhood International Club around the world, without whom this book would not exist.

INTRODUCTION

You are never too old to set another
goal or to dream a new dream.

—C. S. Lewis

As much as advances in science, medicine, and technology have made it possible for large numbers of people to live longer in better health than ever before, no one really considered how extended longevity would affect the human experience as a whole. Even though there is now some awareness of the extent to which living longer will impact all sectors of society, the majority of people still believe that we will just be living in a world with a top-heavy load of old people sitting on the porch, consuming more than their fair share of social services because their pensions are insufficient to support them for an extended period of time.

But this does not have to be the case for the baby boomer generation (1946–1964) who began exiting the workforce in 2012. The baby boomers are the first generation to pass through the retirement threshold in large numbers with sufficient health, wealth, energy, and technology to experience the Third Journey en masse.

Unfortunately, the baby boomers are almost entirely unprepared to make this journey and will suffer greatly unless they are brave enough to seize the opportunity to experience a life that their parents never dreamed of. The challenge for this generation is that they are not satisfied to sit back and simply be senior citizens; regrettably, they were not actually raised to become anything else. Their parents and grandparents taught them to look forward to spending a few dwindling years watching the sun set and doing very little, and when they were younger, this seemed like a grand plan.

No one told them that they would be stronger than expected, need more financial awareness than expected, be more challenged to keep pace with advances in technology than expected, and be more likely to live longer than expected. No one told them that they would still have unemployed children living at home or that they would be the unpaid babysitters and taxi service of their grandchildren. No one told them that they would have to help pave the way for future generations to enjoy a rewarding postwork life at the same time that they are struggling to create one for themselves.

Today, despite the fact that many countries are starting to increase the minimum retirement age again, there is no doubt that *many people will live at least twenty to thirty years in the postwork phase of their lives.*

While some individuals remain self-directed throughout their lives and always know what to do when they find themselves in unfamiliar territory, many experience unexpected challenges in the Third Journey. What ought to be a relaxing, happy time can frequently prove to be an overwhelming, stressful time, when things that were once taken for granted—such as chasing after children, vacuuming the house, or making household repairs—now somehow seem exhausting or boring.

They want to do something more fulfilling but have little idea what to do or how to go about figuring this out. They still want to make a contribution to society but *all the familiar doors appear closed to them.*

But how did this happen?

For the first forty years or so, their adult lives chugged along at a largely predictable pace. Reckless thoughts of writing novels or spending a year in France were quickly dismissed as selfish or foolhardy—the mortgage wasn't going to pay itself, and you couldn't take the kids out of school. Rather than make tough changes in midlife, most baby boomers deferred their dreams to the mythical land of "retirement" or drowned them in a haze of television,[2] watching as much as five to six hours a day.

---

2. "According to Nielsen ratings, boomers watch over nine hours of television a day," *Why Marketers Can't Afford to Ignore Baby Boomers,* the Nielsen Company, Media and Entertainment, last modified July 19, 2010, http://www.nielsen.com/us/en/insights/news/2010/why-marketers-cant-afford-to-ignore-baby-boomers.html.

Now that they have arrived at their postwork lives, they have nothing planned beyond the grocery shopping and a weekly game of golf, and they continue to spend countless hours in front of the television or surfing the web when they might be out having a life.

Talk about escapism; if they continue this television addiction in their postwork years, a person who lives to be eighty will have easily watched *thirty thousand hours* of TV since turning sixty-five[3]—that is a very long time to be sitting in the dark staring at a box!

Retirement Phases

As their work lives progress, everyone knows that their retirement dates are approaching, and the majority of people fall into one of two misguided groups: (1) those who are in outright denial regarding the fact that their lives will change; and (2) those who assume that transitioning out of the workforce and into the third phase of their lives will be a walk in the park.

Some baby boomers do think about their lives after work, but it is amazing just how few people formulate a realistic plan for what they will do with all of their time. When asked what they plan to do when they stop working, some do respond that they plan the trip of a lifetime, but the majority have been financially tied to a job that, at best, they lost interest in a long time ago (or at worst, loathe going to), and their initial postwork plan is literally to sleep in.

But is this sufficient?

You spent your last five or more years at work dreaming of the day you no longer have to be there, and sleep is the best thing you can come up with as an alternative? Okay, maybe for a week or so, but after that, do you really want to find yourself pacing the living room wondering what to do with yourself?

You could watch television to avoid thinking about, or dealing with all the things that you really ought to be getting on with. Or maybe you are more of a Facebook fanatic, or a gym junkie, or a chronic cleaner; it doesn't matter what you are doing. If your sole reason for doing it is to

---

3. Ibid.

fill the day and avoid thinking about having a real life, then it's time to make some changes.

We realize this sounds ridiculous or daunting to many people, but it makes perfect sense once you understand what is actually going on in your mind.[4] The following diagram illustrates the typical person's first year in the postwork world. Initial euphoria generated from simply being free is followed by the joy of doing anything that you were not able to do when working; then suddenly it all stops. This can be experienced to a greater or lesser degree, depending on your personality or circumstances, but most people do hit at least a couple of patches of choppy water:

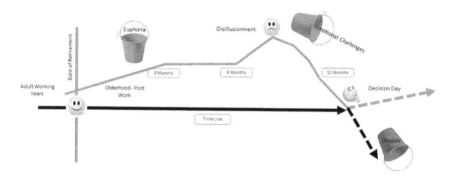

The First Year of Retirement

It can be very hard to accept that your new life plan is not working out as expected and that you might just have to do some work on yourself to alter your circumstances. Some people have worked their entire careers doing one thing, to the point that it defines them, and it is very scary to even begin to think about working to become someone else at the point when you thought you had finally established your self-identity. This misaligned sense of identity can be experienced by doctors, lawyers, plumbers, bus drivers, and anyone else who had to conform to an employer's expectations on a daily basis. For forty years they suited up in

---

4. It goes without saying that not everyone arrives at the Third Journey in the same way or at the same age. The examples in this book will focus on a traditional retirement scenario, but the suggestions and advice can be applied to the majority of circumstances.

their work togs, and they knew who they were. They were skilled, and trusted and needed and sometimes even in positions of great authority—but now what?

Bob Lowry of SatisfyingRetirement.blogspot.com sums it up this way: "The end of a career and the beginning of retirement prompts major changes in your personal identity, use of time, and relationships. If your retirement is not by choice, the stress can be even more disturbing, since losing a job can create an enormous hole in your sense of purpose and self-worth. For most of us, what we've done to earn a living defines us."[5]

Some people think they can simply pretend that nothing is happening, and they will themselves into a state of denial. They will continue to spend money as if they still earned a salary; they will eat junk food, and refuse to be called "Grandma." This "retirement thing" isn't going to get them down—*no siree.* They are going to golf every day, play with their iPads, or go to the mall and have lunch with the girls, just like always.

We call this the *euphoria phase.* They are so delighted to not be chained to a desk, or an assembly line, or a delivery schedule that blissful days of Netflix and nothingness seem like life in heaven. Sometimes they even embark on a new hobby, like golf or scrapbooking, and at first the uninterrupted hours to pursue this latent passion seem a godsend.

But then one day about six months after leaving their jobs, right on the cusp of the ninth tee, they look out over a cloudless sky and catch themselves wondering something quite unsettling: "Is this all there is?"

They shudder and do their best to shake it off, of course, but the bubble has burst. We call this the *disillusionment phase.*

And then they notice something really disconcerting—their friends have started to drift away. Some move to warmer climates or to be closer to grandchildren; others move to condos or start caring for a relative. Then they wake up one morning and realize that they no longer know anyone on the street where they have lived for forty years, and it hits them—*they* might have avoided changing, but everyone around them has changed and left them behind.

To make matters worse, in the absence of workweek commitments and

5. "I'm Retired So Who am I Now?" Bob Lowry, *Next Avenue*, accessed November 13, 2012, http://www.nextavenue.org/im-retired-so-who-am-i-now.

events, married postwork couples frequently discover that they no longer have anything in common with the person with whom they share a house. Not only do they barely recognize the person sitting across from them at the breakfast table, but that person is starting to really annoy them. Being constantly reminded that the dishwasher does not unload itself or that they seem to have gained weight really does not make things better.

Welcome to the *free fall phase* of your postwork life, where everyone around you seems to be speaking a foreign language and everything seems to cost twice as much as you thought it would. It might not be so bad if you had any idea how far you were going to fall, how and where you were going to land, what the risk of getting injured was, or whether you were being jettisoned into hostile territory. Without proper planning, you can become agitated, stressed, and depressed—and in extreme circumstances, this can even lead to serious health complications that ultimately further impact your ability to enjoy your Third Journey.

You might get through this difficult phase unscathed if you had a parachute and some landing skills, but you don't—you didn't need them; this retirement thing was going to be a piece of cake.

"Well, who needs a parachute? I've been a grown-up for forty-five years."

"Bad news—you have been an Oldster for about five minutes, and all the rules have changed."

"But that is insane."

"Nope. All those years you were busy working or running the house, you essentially made a deal with yourself—you would show up to work on time and more or less behave and conform to the rules. And in return, you would get money and vacations in Florida and eventually a golden retirement."

"Everyone knows that."

"Indeed they do. Now answer a simple question for me: what is your job now and who is paying you to behave?"

"No one. I don't have a job. I'm retired!"

"Exactly. So what is your purpose now, and what are you getting in return for cooperating?"

⇔

Without a meaningful purpose, during the initial phase of your postwork life, you run the risk of throwing your life completely out of balance because the anticipated thrill of embarking on a long journey is all that has been supporting you. Now that the bloom is off the rose, so to speak, the doer inside you is about to throw a fit.

"What's a doer?"

"It is the part of you that hums when you are doing something you enjoy. Up until this point you have done a pretty good job keeping it busy—raising kids, mowing the lawn, running a multinational conglomerate. It doesn't care as long as it is doing something. The problem is, it requires constant activity, or it starts to get bored, and when it gets bored, it starts inventing ways to fill the void: overeating, sulking, drinking, picking fights, plotting to take over the world. It doesn't care as long as it has something entertaining to while away the hours."

The strength of the doer inside you is a reflection on your self-worth—the more you believe that you can still make a valuable contribution, the more you will continue to drive yourself to accomplish things to maintain it.

Let's be clear about this. We are not suggesting that all retired people should be working seven days a week—far from it. We are merely suggesting that by the time people reach the postwork phase of their lives, their personalities are sufficiently formed that they are unconsciously negotiating with themselves all the time regarding what to do next. If you can work out this unconsciously, then why not step up to the plate and do it on purpose? Why not finally make an agreement with yourself to *do something that has meaning for you* and that you will find fulfilling, thereby experiencing things like peace, contentment, and (dare we say it?) happiness?

Not everyone who reads this book will be at the same point in his or her journey or be in any way like the typical retiree that we reference. But regardless of what brought this book into your hands, what follows is an opportunity to learn how to plan, structure, and implement the third phase of your life in such a way that it meets more of your expectations, goals, and dreams, and to pick up a few ideas, thoughts, and strategies for navigating the challenges that you may face.

Does all this sound a bit daunting, idealistic, or unrealistic? Don't worry; just keep reading, and we'll figure it out together.

CHAPTER 1

The First Year of Your New Life

Chance favors the prepared mind.
—Louis Pasteur

The first year on the other side of the retirement threshold is easy for some, difficult for others, and different for everyone. It is a big transition, and as part of that transition you need to uncover your fears and emotions, and embrace the choices you have.

Therefore, the critical factor you *must* address is that change is indeed upon you. This is not a rehearsal of life; this is it. If you don't recognize that change is in your hands and that you simply must handle it and make decisions, then you will inevitably fall into a slow-paced, static, sedentary lifestyle. You will become used to boredom and restlessness, and—perhaps most importantly—it will slowly damage your body beyond repair. A few extra pounds here and there, a few extra glasses of wine, only a little bit of exercise, and a sleep-in day each week will all mount up.

Welcome to the Roller Coaster

When people first pass through the threshold from the work world to the rest of their lives, most have some sort of expectation of what things will look like on the other side; but few expect to find themselves sitting in a roller-coaster car. The ride begins with a slow uphill climb, as expected, and there is even a moment or two to pause and enjoy the sunny view from the top.

Suddenly, without warning, the car plunges down into a dark tunnel, where things prove to be more different than expected. Being seasoned travelers, most people don't panic, assuming that they will be back in the sunshine very soon.

But this metaphorical roller coaster has another destination, and before you know what has happened, you find yourself deep inside a carnival fun house, where the roof threatens to cave in on you, and unseen hands grab your sleeve from the left and right. What is most unnerving is that everyone seems to want something from you or to tell you what to do, and the whole experience makes you increasingly uneasy.

It does not seem to matter whether you were looking forward to being a glorified couch potato or whether you were dreading the endless hours around the house. Something that you can't quite put your finger on is making you very irritable, and there is just no pleasing you. When you are alone, you crave company, and when the relatives come over, you grimace and go hide in the den.

If you are like most of us, you get out of bed every day with the intention of keeping things on an even keel, but it doesn't always turn out that way. The purpose of this book is to offer some suggestions as to how to make your postwork journey look more like the following diagram:

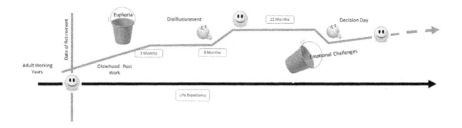

Your Third Journey

Up until now, you have navigated through life using a set of lifestyle morals and principles that were either passed down to you by your parents or acquired independently through your own life experiences. If you are blissfully happy with your current situation, and your future is assured, close this book and walk away. We have no desire to wake you from the dream life that most Oldsters are still seeking.

However, if you are having a slightly uncomfortable thought that this might not be what you really want, then perhaps there are a few ideas in here that might prove useful.

We'll let you be the judge.

But before you do, consider the following: the way that human life is structured all over the planet. Every fiber of your being is conditioned to participate in an endless uphill climb throughout your first fifty years or so. There are goals to set, responsibilities to meet, children to raise, and promotions to acquire. Regardless of your culture, ethnicity, or religion, great pains are taken to equip you with the life skills that you need to make this initial journey.

But traditional retirement life presents itself as the antithesis of this; everything is geared toward winding down, managing some degree of failing physical functionality, and accepting diminished mental capacity. Except for financial planning, there is no universal standard or source of collective wisdom for planning a successful second fifty years. The universal, generally accepted mantra seems to be, "Enjoy your time as you can, and accept your circumstance. You are old, and you are just going to get older."

It all seems so futile, and for a lot of people it is, because modern society has lulled us into a submissive state where we are conditioned to accept and expect that once we pass the age of sixty-five, we begin a long, slow slide into oblivion.

Considering Your Options

What can you do to prepare if you are not yet retired?

Should you consider embarking on a second career?

What can you do if you are already in the postwork phase of your life, and you are determined to reject the notion that everything is downhill from here on?

And so we say again: the only thing you really should be pondering with regard to the postwork phase of life is whether you are going to sink into the golden age of so-called decay or willfully choose the road not yet taken and embark on your Third Journey in defiance of yourself, your circumstances, and advice from well-intentioned family members.

"So why bother?" you might ask.

"Well, what if you are a scientist, sitting on the cure for cancer, but you don't know that yet, and you never find out because you stopped going to the lab because your knees ached a bit, and you didn't like riding the bus?"

"That's ridiculous."

"No, it isn't. Just because a company or a government retired you does not mean that you have fulfilled your purpose as a person or that you have accomplished your mission."

"But I am sixty-five years old!"

"Well, then, you'd better get moving in a hurry if you want to get everything done in time!"

Okay, so we exaggerate a little to make a point, but the following list definitely proves that you are never too old to accomplish something amazing. As you read, consider what the world might be like if these people had given up, just because they were older:

- Benjamin Franklin signed the American Declaration of Independence at the age of seventy.
- Nelson Mandela became president of South Africa at the age of seventy-six.
- Mother Teresa was sixty-nine when she received the Nobel Peace Prize.
- Grandma Moses did not start painting until she was seventy-six and kept right on going until she died at the age of 101.
- At the age of one hundred, Ralph Waldo McBurney published his first novel, titled *My First 100 Years*. He lived to the age of 106 and was considered to be the oldest worker in America at that time.
- At fifty-five, Pablo Picasso completed his masterpiece *Guernica*.

- At fifty-six, Mao Zedong founded the People's Republic of China.
- At fifty-eight, Sony chairman Akio Morita introduced the Sony Walkman and changed the music industry forever.
- At fifty-nine, "Satchel" Paige became the oldest Major League baseball player.
- At sixty-two, J. R. R. Tolkien published the first volume of his fantasy series, *The Lord of the Rings.*
- At sixty-five, jazz musician Miles Davis performed his final live album, just weeks before he died.
- At sixty-eight, the English experimentalist Sir William Crookes began investigating radioactivity and invented a device for detecting alpha particles.
- At seventy, Cornelius Vanderbilt began buying railroads.
- At seventy-one, Katsusuke Yanagisawa, a retired Japanese schoolteacher, became the oldest person to climb Mount Everest.
- At seventy-seven, John Glenn became the oldest person to go into space.
- At seventy-eight, Chevalier de Lamarck proposed a new theory of the evolutionary process, claiming that acquired characteristics can be transmitted to offspring.
- At seventy-nine, Asa Long became the oldest US checkers champion.
- At eighty-two, William Ivy Baldwin became the oldest tightrope walker, crossing the South Boulder Canyon in Colorado on a 320-foot wire.
- At eighty-eight, Michelangelo created the architectural plans for the Church of Santa Maria.
- At ninety, Marc Chagall became the first living artist to be exhibited at the Louvre museum.
- At ninety-three, P. G. Wodehouse worked on his ninety-seventh novel and was knighted.
- At ninety-four, comedian George Burns performed in Schenectady, New York, sixty-three years after his first performance there.
- At ninety-five, Nola Ochs became the oldest person to receive a college diploma.

Case Study: *Is Early Retirement Everything They Tell You?*

Barry had been an executive manager for most of his business life. He worked for a multinational company and was based in one location but traveled to subsidiary companies and clients around the world. He was certainly well compensated, and when he was at home, mainly on weekends, he loved to play golf. As he was crossing over the sixty-year mark, he really began to feel that the pressure of work, travel, and client dinners was taking its toll on him. He was tired and drained and decided to accept a lucrative early retirement package.

At his leaving party, he excitedly announced, "I am really looking forward to playing more golf, especially during the week when the course is quieter. I reckon two days during the week, plus I'll keep my Saturday date with our usual foursome. So far so good."

The first three months were wonderful. He was free at last and was thoroughly enjoying his own space. Yet by month four he was already craving something more to do. He still loved being on the fairways, to be sure, but the "afterlife," as he called it, was not working out as he had envisaged it.

"Financially, I'm secure for life, and I will easily leave a good level of money to the kids, but I don't feel fulfilled. Maybe I do miss the razzmatazz of the office life after all. I don't honestly think so, to be honest, but I'm not as occupied mentally as I expected to be. Although, in fairness to myself, I don't think I gave much thought to the intellectual side of life. I was probably almost entirely consumed with fresh air and golf balls."

So what's his advice?

"If you can, stay working for as long as you can. Retirement is a great idea, but in this day and age where we are healthier and, in theory, at least younger, then age sixty, as I was, is just too early in one's personal evolution to retreat from the world. Maybe I should have stuck it out a few years longer or at least thought over the decision to leave work for longer than I did."

Barry is now in his fifth year of retirement. He still plays golf but only twice a week, once at the weekend. He managed to get some part-time consulting work that keeps him busy for a good part of the week and encourages him to keep up-to-date with what is going on in his industry, which satisfies his need for mental stimulation.

Unraveling the Mess

The hardest thing to do when you first leave the work world is to realize that all of your old dog-eat-dog work habits have followed you home, and they are in the process of messing up your shiny new life.

As you pass through the retirement threshold into the postwork world, there are certain things you expect to collect: your retirement gift, your pension plan information, your bus pass, and your freedom. But there is something else that clings to your shoe as you pass through the retirement threshold that very few people expect—your personal stuff.

Think of this as your own invisible, knotted-up ball of negativity, composed of all the accumulated fears, weaknesses, vices, and regrets that have built up inside you during the first half of your life. If you are some sort of a Zen master, your ball of stuff might be as small as a marble, but if you have been careless with yourself, it might be as large as a bale of hay. Either way, you have no choice but to carry it with you on your Third Journey, like an invisible ball and chain, unless you decide to do something about it.

As should be clearly understood, we are not medical professionals, and there are some problems that definitely require professional assistance to resolve. Having said that, if you view your lifetime of accumulated blockages as a knotted ball of twine, then you will realize that regardless of how large or how tangled it is, you can begin to gently unravel it with outside help, if needed, but you can at least make some progress on your own.

LIFE BEGINS
AT
RETIREMENT

In time, if you stick at it, you will be surprised just how much progress you can make, both in unraveling the deeply buried fears and prejudices that you know have always held you back and, more important, in beginning to understand some of your deeper weaknesses that you never realized were driving your decision-making processes.

As you read the later chapters of this book, you will see that we have tackled all the subjects and situations that you are likely to confront, and we offer some insights regarding how to break them down into bite-size pieces.

Everyone tells you it is time to downsize, organize, and clean out the closets when you retire—the physical collections. But why is it that no one stresses the importance of clearing out all the mental baggage that you have been dragging around in your psyche?

You may need to think about this issue for a little while and self-analyze many areas unique to you. So in the meantime, let's figure out how well you know yourself. Get a pencil and complete the following sentences, using your personal circumstances as a reference. Go ahead, and write the very first thing the pops into your head as you do this (we promise not to peek!).

Okay, ready?

- When I was ten, I was the best one in my class at _____
- When I was in high school, everyone knew me as a _____
- When I worked, my job was to _____

- Now that I am free to do anything, my job is to _____
- My project for the rest of my life is to _____

"Whoa, there … what's this stuff about a job? I just retired five minutes ago. I have earned the right to take it easy!"

"*Easy*? Did you ever stop to ask yourself if you actually want to be idle?"

"What?"

"Are you sure that you are ever going to be happy watching the world rush by when you could be doing something useful with your time?"

Developing a New Purpose

Think about it this way: up until the moment you stopped working, you were fully employed doing a job, running a household, raising a family, or meeting deadlines. Unless you are already a master planner with a detailed road map for the rest of your life, the moment you passed through the retirement threshold, *you ceased to have a clear purpose*, and the world around you began treating you as if you were no longer useful.

You might still be interested in making a traditional work contribution, but more than likely the workforce is no longer interested in you; they have traded you in for a shiny new genius with a computer strapped to his wrist, and there is not a moment to lose if you want to avoid that downhill plunge into the darkness.

The feeling that you are creeping toward the end of life may seem overwhelming, or you may choose simply to ignore this fear and get on with living your life. The best practice is to recognize aches and pains as they arise, and while they must be considered for health reasons, don't classify them as signals that it is time to give up. Clearly, if there are medical issues, then take all necessary advice and precautions, but leaving that aside, life after retirement is not in a holding pattern. It is the time to refresh your thinking, your ideas, your plans, and your lifestyle.

Face this reality and decide on a purpose for your new life as soon as you are able to do so.[6] It is okay if you change your purpose as you progress, but the moment you cease to have one, it is the same as being out of work. The longer you let things slide, the harder it will be to get back to work. This is a situation you need to avoid at all costs, because the more you fall into despair the more likely you are to develop a chronic health condition brought on by stress.

Once the idea of rethinking and restructuring takes hold, the retirement lifestyle will evolve into a very exciting time of your life. Yes, you can travel and see places you always wanted to visit, and yes, you can do more gardening, but the fundamental change you will experience is that all decisions about lifestyle are now made by *you*, not by a boss (spouse aside!) and not determined by some company policies and procedures. If you want to eat dinner at 4:00 p.m. or Skype with the Philippines at 3:00 a.m., so be it.

The freedom-of-choice issue is like a light going on in your mind.

You can—and inevitably will—be influenced by other people, friends, family, peers, and so forth. You will be influenced by money, weather, politics, and social factors, but everyday decisions are all yours to make. This can be a double-edged sword in that the more freedom you actually have, the more daunting the task of making choices can be, and not everyone handles this well.

Establishing a Routine

This emancipation is a sea change in most people's retirement lives. It is fascinating to realize that you can choose to do things you perhaps never even thought of, and you don't have to discuss or consult with anyone else, and most importantly, you probably don't have to seek permission.

You only have to give yourself permission to truly love living free.

Yet adapting to a self-decision lifestyle can be challenging for many people. It would be too offensive to suggest that some people go through life, particularly in the working years, following the *instructions* of others—from employers, spouses, or, for that matter, even children. Many people find running a household or creating a personal budget a

---

6. If you don't know how to decide on a purpose, check out chapter 14.

challenge. They literally stumble from one paycheck to another and hope that the bank doesn't call about being overdrawn. Yet in retirement, the paycheck safety net has disappeared. Now, you have decisions to make about money and, in turn, about what you want to do with this newfound freedom—and whether you can afford it.

The entire retirement lifestyle structure is so different from the fairly static structure of life during the working years. The weekday routine was the same, day after day, week after week, in the main. "Taking a break" typically meant taking a break from that routine and getting some fresh air. However, the following week you were back into the same old routine all over again. If your employer said, "We start at nine o'clock," then you needed to be onsite at nine o'clock. If that is what you experienced, then you probably were living in a regular pattern, where external issues or influences played a significant part. But now, in retirement, if you get out of bed at eight o'clock, fine, or if you choose to get out of bed at ten o'clock, then equally fine; the decision is entirely yours. No one else is involved.

Society conditions us to have preconceived notions about life in retirement—lots of free time, playing golf a few times every week, endless travel, work around the house, more time with the grandkids, and so forth. But the biggest change you feel is the realization that you are now *in* the latter years, and even though you've known for years that when you finally left the work world, you would be in your older years, this can still be a traumatic realization.

Even if you are open to living differently, how can you embark on the journey of a lifetime if you have not been mentally prepared for it? How can you make sensible decisions if you have not researched your options? These questions often become fears that give birth to indecision and procrastination.

Undoubtedly, this is a situation when chance definitely favors the prepared; it is never a good idea to delay making changes, no matter how uncomfortable it may be. Making pivotal changes in the first year of your retirement can set you up for success in the years to come.

Top Ten Tips for Your Journey

1. Your first year in the postwork world is seldom what you expect.
2. Don't think retired; think new beginnings.
3. If you don't do it now, you probably never will.
4. If you feel you haven't lived thus far, start now.
5. You really must *plan* your retirement happiness.
6. Do things that *you* want to do.
7. Don't mimic your peers; do the things that bring satisfaction to you.
8. Don't stop wanting to learn.
9. Unravel your ball of stuff one knot at a time.
10. Think young, but act your age.

PSYCHOLOGICAL ASPECTS OF RETIREMENT

The Influence of Psychomotivation

Stop trying to leave and you will arrive. Stop seeking, and
you will see. Stop running away and you will be found.

—Lao Tzu

In this chapter we will discuss the importance of recognizing that the
better your reason for getting out of bed in the morning, the more
likely you are to keep getting up and moving forward. In doing so, we
introduce the term *psychomotivation*—a concept that we will refer to often
throughout the book.

Psychomotivation is an all-embracing phrase to convey the notion
that what we do is largely, if not totally, controlled by how we feel about
doing it. In simple terms, it means that anything we do in our lives,
most especially in our latter years, and the ability to succeed at it is
totally dependent on whether we have reason to do it. There must be an
incentive of some sort, a benefit that can be gained—a purpose. If there
is no reason to do something, then, especially as we age, the feeling of
"why bother?" increases.

Psychomotivation is a very personal part of everyone's life. One
person's motivation is not another person's motivation, and truth be told,
most of us make decisions based on an ever-changing set of priorities.
Some of these things are life-affirming, and some are self-defeating; the

more we can acknowledge that our experiences in the Third Journey will depend on our choices, the more we can choose a path that makes us happy.

Moreover, what motivates you to think about a situation, or handle a problem, or just get the job done will, in all probability, not motivate anyone else. Even telling friends about *your* motivation will have little, if any, impact and far less appreciation on *their* motivation. Likewise, their motivation will not cause you to change yours or even recognize that it could make a difference in your life. Emotions and feelings are highly personal and are rarely experienced by other people in the same situation in the same way.

Now, we're willing to bet you have no shortage of determination and can do just about anything you set your mind to do, but the idea of setting a realistic goal, breaking it down into a series of manageable steps, and actually seeing it through might seem a bit daunting for some. But not to worry; that is what this book is for.

We will also discuss how to identify and unravel all the stuff in your subconscious that you have been using to hold yourself back and how to convert these challenges into opportunities to make small or major changes at any point in your life.

The Big Myth

One of the New Age theories of existence focuses on the notion that the biggest problem people face when they get to "retirement heaven" is realizing that they have indeed arrived, because it initially looks exactly like the world they just left. In some respects, the start of your Third Journey is frequently a lot like this. You go to sleep one night, a member of the workforce, and wake up the next morning in a new and foreign land. Yes, you know you have retired because your daily schedule has changed, but in all other respects, life seems to be pretty much the same, and so you assume it is and go about your daily activities in the same way.

Big mistake.

Ironically, modern society places significant emphasis on the constant changes that take place during the first third of our lives—our bodies grow, we learn, we develop personalities, and we form relationships and a sense of ourselves—but also encourages us to believe that very few changes take place during the last third of our lives. However, advances in longevity mean that this is far from the case, and determining personal psychomotivation increasingly becomes the difference between falling apart and thriving in your third journey.

People joke about having a second childhood, but very few people appreciate just how appropriate this term is for the phase that everyone goes through when they first pass through the retirement threshold. Your first days at home are often quite euphoric, and it is not unusual to feel a rush of exhilaration unlike anything you have experienced in years, making you prone to silly, giggly actions—you eat ice cream in the middle of the day, you go around with your shirt on backward, you color at the kitchen table with the grandkids, you buy yourself a shiny new toy.

The early days are also the stage for some remarkable temper tantrums over seemingly small things as you dust off and release some of your pent-up work-world frustration. You chop down trees that block your view, you shred boxes of documents no longer needed, you throw all your business suits in a heap in the middle of the floor and stomp on them, and you pick a fight with the family dog for stealing your spot on the sofa—good times, indeed.

To say you are acting out is an understatement, but no one addresses it. Instead, there are hushed voices in the corridor ...

"Now, just give him a little time to get his bearings ... make sure you play quietly outside. Grandpa is trying to rest."

Perfect. You have just been released from forty years of hard labor, and now your parole officer (a.k.a. your spouse) is sentencing you to a nap. To keep the peace, you grudgingly comply, but just when you are getting settled, she will stick her head through the doorway to verify that you have, in fact, stayed where she put you. She attempts to justify this by demanding to know whether you want a cup of tea. There is no right answer to this, of course; if you decline, she'll be back in ten minutes to ask if you are sure, and if you accept, she will be back in seventeen minutes with coffee—she wasn't in the mood for tea.

That's okay, though; you have a secret way of getting even. The next time she announces that she is going to do the grocery shopping, wait until she picks up the car keys and then leap off the sofa and ask,

WILLIAM R. STORIE AND ROBIN W. TRIMINGHAM

"Can I come?" This will drive her completely insane because she is still struggling to work out why this mundane errand that she used to loathe is suddenly feeling like a refuge from a life sentence of togetherness.

If you really want to see your spouse go nuts, when you get to the store, stroll up and down the aisles and make random comments regarding where you would stock the toilet paper, and start little debates regarding which brand of peas should be purchased for that yummy tuna casserole she insists on making again. You don't need to worry about offending or annoying each other—there won't be any conversation in the car on the way home anyway because you each cannot tolerate the way the other one drives.

Don't worry if you don't win the battle today. The best part about your postwork life is that there is absolutely nothing to prevent you both from getting up tomorrow and doing the same thing all over again.

Still sure that there is no such thing as a second childhood? Don't kid yourself—there is a naughty, selfish seven-year-old inside you who has been waiting for years for an opportunity to act out. Your lack of planning has given him plenty of free time to invent nasty new games for you to play.

Reality Sets In

If that was all you had to contend with, you would probably be fine, but you are just getting started. Sooner or later, your inner child will get bored with these silly games, and you will make the mistake of taking a good look in the mirror. If you can still see clearly, this is usually followed by a silent gasp as you catch yourself thinking, *When did I get so old?*

This bone-chilling experience is all the worse in the Western world, where youth and beauty rule, and a twenty-nine-year-old can be labeled over the hill. Clearly, it is time for some sort of evasive action.

Ironically, most people respond in one of two ways: they either give up because aging is an unavoidable battle that they just can't win, or they go on a crash diet and attempt to inject themselves with enough Botox to turn into mannequins. In both cases, their daily lives become consumed by an overconcentration on external physical factors, to the complete detriment of their internal emotional, intellectual, and spiritual well-being. Some might argue that the Botox beauties look good in photographs, but they are nothing more than hollow beings in pretty suits. What these Oldsters miss is the opportunity to embrace their years of experience to *rejuvenate themselves on the inside* by discovering what motivates them most deeply and mobilizing their core skills to push themselves in new ways.

QUIET THE MIND
AND THE SOUL WILL SPEAK
Ma Jaya Sati Bhagavati

Clearing Your First Hurdle

The biggest hurdle that these Oldsters face is the fear that from here on in, they are just going to lose their ability to do more and more things, and no matter what they do, they will wither to the point that they are unable to care for themselves. Aging literally becomes their excuse for not living, when it should be only one of a range of factors that is considered when making lifestyle decisions. There is a certain sense of peace of mind that comes from being able to accept your limitations without allowing them to define your existence.

There is no question that it is uncomfortable to acknowledge, let alone discuss, the changes that continue to take place as we age because of the inevitable negative aspects of decline and eventually mortality. But continually vacillating between apathy and impatience impedes people from addressing all the other changes that take place inside them that might make the Third Journey enjoyable, even transformative, if they only paid attention.

So what's the answer?

That depends on at what point you are in your life at the present moment.

Getting Going

If you are reading this at any point *before* retirement, realize that you will be facing an uphill climb the moment you pass through the threshold into the postwork world, so start training for the journey now.

If you are reading this at any point *after* having passed through the retirement threshold, realize that you are facing a steeper climb, but it is never too late to start. Yes, you might be seventy-two or eighty-two, but you can still create positive psychomotivations for yourself by embracing new opportunities. There is no wrong time to make your first trip to Italy, take photography classes, or meet your first great-grandchild. You just need to have a clear goal in mind, good planning, and a good dose of determination (that's code for bullheaded stubbornness). Psychomotivations are entirely personal; there is no template for living. Your reasons for thriving in retirement are entirely of your own making.

Case Study: *Is it harder to be forced into early retirement than to leave work on your own?*

Judy was a special education teacher in Sydney, Australia. At the age of sixty-two, she was shocked to receive the news that her position was being made redundant when her school was amalgamated with a larger one in the area. This came as an unexpected shock that she initially found difficult to reconcile because she was not ready to replace her work motivation with a new nonwork motivation.

"People just aren't having as many children as they used to," says Judy. "Enrollment had been down for some time, and I guess I should have seen it coming, but it was a real shock, I'll tell you. Looking back, I guess it was to be expected, but when it happened, it was a serious blow.

"The impact on my savings and pension plan was pretty heavy, but luckily, my husband is still working, so overall we're reasonably fine financially. But the trauma that it caused me personally and professionally was really bad. Given my age, it was impossible to find another position, and I really took that to heart. It made me believe that I had been useless at my job for all these years and that I was being cast aside. It has caused me endless number of sleepless nights about feeling inferior and washed up. My husband says I should just get over it and get on with my life, but I can't. I really loved my job, and I don't want to do anything else."

These days, Judy's life is taken up with some volunteer work to fill the hours and running after four grandchildren she adores. While she has found renewed vitality in life, this did not come to her without considerable adjustment.

Top Ten Tips for Your Journey

1. This is the start of your new life; embrace it.
2. Doing what *you* want to do is a learning exercise.
3. You are not over the hill—you can climb as long as you believe you can continue to climb.
4. If you feel you haven't lived thus far, you probably haven't, so start now.
5. Seek reasons to do new things.
6. Don't be controlled by the "why bother?" attitude.
7. Get out of bed every morning—that's always a good start.
8. Don't rest on past glories. This is a new life. Do new things.
9. Remember yesterday, but never imagine you can live there.
10. Think young, but act your age.

CHAPTER 3

Factors Affecting Longevity

Once you eliminate the impossible, whatever remains,
no matter how improbable, must be the truth.
—Arthur Conan Doyle

In this chapter we will discuss developing a balance between longevity, health, and the will to live. There is a tendency, upon reaching retirement, for your life to fall out of balance if you start worrying that you are running out of time on earth, simply because you think that you will never be useful again. In essence, you become obsessed with the notion that clocks don't run backward, to the point that you forget to look forward.

Longevity

It is true to say that most people would like to live forever if they could just figure out how to avoid getting old. The goal of longevity is certainly of high importance to younger people, especially if they are raising families, working, and making good money. It is also a goal of Oldsters, but the reality of a long life and its attendant issues, such as health, financial worries, boredom, and loneliness, is that the appeal of longevity frequently diminishes with age.

Unfortunately, none of us knows how long we actually have to live—or perhaps, fortunately. Scientists have concluded that the typical human body *can* live for 120[7] years, but a huge range of factors affects and challenges the likelihood that we will reach this age over the course of our lifetimes. This makes it difficult to complete every single thing we wanted to do in our Third Journey, but should we really let this stop us from implementing a plan and running with it?

Absolutely not.

Generally speaking, everyone starts life with an equal chance of winning the "longevity lottery," and even if your health is poor, there will always be those who defy the odds and recover. There is no reason to assume that you cannot be one of them.[8]

But let's think about this for a minute. Have you ever wondered what it would be like to live to be more than one hundred years old? Even in this age of modern medicine, it seems an unlikely goal for most, yet some people seem to get there with very little effort.

The United Nations predicts that there will be 2.2 million people over the age of one hundred by the year 2050,[9] making the idea of universal longevity a real possibility for the first time in human evolution.

How can that possibly be?

Scientists are not completely sure whether genes or lifestyle is the greatest influence on longevity, but the latest research is pointing to some surprisingly simple factors. For example, on the remote Greek island of Ikaria,[10] people frequently live beyond the age of ninety, because the community as a whole has adopted a natural easygoing appreciation

---

7. It is generally accepted that the first person to live to the age of 150 has already been born. Kate Kelland, "Who Wants to Live Forever? Scientists See Aging Cured," *Reuters*, accessed July 4, 2011, http://www.reuters.com/article/us-ageing-cure-idUSTRE7632ID20110704.

8. A family member of one of the authors of this book, who, at age sixty, was given a few days to live, went on to live until age ninety-six. Amazing. He had reconciled with his impending departure and had no dreams or aspirations of living beyond next week. He was at peace. The notion that he would live and live well for another thirty-six years was the most astonishing thing in his life—and that of his family.

9. Matthew Bandyk, "The Future of the Economy: 2050," *US News*, accessed February 2, 2010, http://www.usnews.com.

10. For a general overview of Icaria, see https://en.wikipedia.org/wiki/Icaria.

of life itself. According to the author of *Ikaria*, Diane Kochilas, whose family resides on the island, the Icarians literally "forget to die." They also apparently "forget to get sick" and experience very little cancer, cardiovascular disease, or dementia.[11] These people don't claim any genetic advantage, but they do adhere to a mostly vegetarian diet, and they live with an unhurried appreciation of life itself.

As a matter of habit, the Icarians also walk everywhere, take afternoon naps, use herbs to treat simple ailments, and love to dance. To these people, life is an experience to be savored, and bad feelings and negativity are little more than a waste of time.

Health

Leaving genetics aside for a moment, the greatest determining factor in how long and how fully you will be able to experience the Third Journey that is almost completely within your control is the state of your overall health.

Ancient wisdom would have us believe that you have the ability to heal yourself, but modern science would say that most people only reach old age because prescription medicines help them to survive in spite of the presence of multiple diseases and dependencies.

Who is right?

Would you believe both are correct?

According to a new study conducted by Newcastle University's Institute for Aging and Keio University School of Medicine, Tokyo, which investigated factors contributing to the ability to live to be one hundred, the ability to keep inflammation levels low inside your body contributes greatly to your ability to live to be extremely old, making a strong case to assume that chronic inflammation negatively affects human aging.[12]

Simply put, chronic inflammation is one of the key contributors

---

11. Diane Kochilas, *Ikaria: Lessons on Food, Life, and Longevity from the Greek Island Where People Forget to Die* (New York: Rodale, 2014), xi.

12. "Inflammation, but not telomere length, predicts successful ageing at extreme old age: a longitudinal study of semi-supercentenarians," *EBioMedicine* 2, no. 10 (October 2015), http://www.ebiomedicine.com/article/S2352-3964(15)30081-5/fulltext.

to many diseases of the elderly, including diabetes, Alzheimer's, heart attack, colon cancer, and diseases of the bones and joints. The research would indicate that by keeping inflammation down (which contributes to keeping your health in balance), anyone can succeed in fighting off diseases longer in life and—are you ready for it?—live independently with good cognition until extreme old age.

But there is a catch. At the present time, "available potent anti-inflammatories are not suited for long-term treatment of chronic inflammation because of their strong side-effects."[13] Scientists are hopeful that this research can be used to begin to develop safer long-term anti-inflammatory drugs that will improve the quality and duration of everyone's life, but until such drugs are introduced, people will have to find another way to control inflammation inside their bodies. Clearly, chronic inflammation is not a good thing, and simply suppressing it with anti-inflammatory drugs and pain killers is not the answer because these drugs just mask the symptoms and do not address the underlying problem that caused the inflammation in the first place.[14]

Self-Health Care

But that does not mean that there is nothing you can do. Reducing the amount of fat in your body by exercising for thirty minutes a day and flossing your teeth to combat gum disease will both assist in reducing inflammation.

Believe it or not, studies have shown[15] that adopting an anti-inflammatory diet (otherwise known as a Mediterranean diet) is one of the best ways to decrease inflammation. The primary components of this eating plan include eating foods rich in omega-3 fatty acids, such as fish, plenty of fruits and vegetables, green tea, whole grains and brown rice, and lean protein, such as chicken; and minimizing all processed foods, trans fats, polyunsaturated fats, carbohydrates that contain gluten (such

---

13. Ibid.

14. For a detailed explanation of inflammation, see chapter 6.

15. Christopher Cannon and Elizabeth Vierck, *Complete Idiot's Guide to the Anti-Inflammation Diet* (New York: Penguin, 2006), 12.

as white bread and white rice), red meat, and full-fat dairy products.[16] For flavor, foods are seasoned with spices such as turmeric, rosemary, ginger, and curry, which also have anti-inflammatory properties.

The other thing that you can do to help to extend your life is to train your brain to expect to live longer and to enjoy being old. In Western culture, where there is an overemphasis on youth, people are raised to believe that they are middle-aged at forty, old at sixty, and should die by the time they are eighty. But if your biological potential is actually 120 years, you will not even reach middle age until you are sixty, and you will not begin to be old until you are at least ninety.

According to Philip Rose, author of *The 120 Club: Living the Good Life for 120 Years*, the key to living to an extremely old age is simply to believe that this can be a reality. He recommends that you tell yourself every day that it is possible to live to be 120. It is the intention that makes the reality possible.

Generally speaking, it is a fair assumption that if they could maintain their health, most people would opt for *more* years rather than *fewer* years in their Third Journey. There is a certain pride in being old, and if you are older than people think you are, even the most reserved, humble person responds favorably to the compliment.

That being said, there are also some nasty self-defeating little games that we play with ourselves when we don't feel that the world is paying enough attention to us at our advanced age. We ignore our doctors' good advice, we smoke, we drink (even though we are on multiple medications), we eat deep-fried food, and we insist on going up to clean the roof, even though we know we get dizzy spells. We can most effectively regain control over these tendencies by actively seeking ways to curb our cravings for these secret little addictions.

The Will to Live

Everyone wants to live as long as possible—as long as they have something to live for. The challenge is to keep coming up with a purpose for being here, once your initial, or early stage, "mission" is fulfilled. For example,

---

16. Ibid., 74.

the family has now grown and moved away, or for some reason the mission is no longer possible. You can't climb Mount Everest if you no longer have the stamina. Many elderly people miraculously keep right on going because they have created an *unending* reason for them to get out of bed in the morning.

Conversely, there comes a point in many people's lives when they say, "I just don't want to live anymore."

Harsh words, perhaps, but true in many cases. Whether through poor health or poor living conditions or being too lonely, many people face the fact that they want to go—and go soon. "I've done what I came here to do, so let me go." If you are presently feeling this way, find someone you trust to talk to—a good place to start is with a therapist, pastor, relative, or friend. Getting old and infirm and mentally challenged can be the primary reasons for wanting the days to come to an end, but there are many others, including becoming a burden—physically and carewise—to the family or society; running out of money and/or health insurance; not being able to leave a large inheritance for family because you had to burn through it; for the vain, looking old and wrinkly, or just becoming utterly bored and lonely and tired of the changing world and life in general. Many older people suffer from chronic anxiety and stress and need to seek constructive ways to release this negative energy on a regular basis. If you are physically strong enough, there is nothing like mowing the lawn, chopping wood, washing windows, or cleaning out the closet under the stairs for burning negative energy in a positive fashion. Not into housework? Try ice skating or dancing or Tai Chi—anything that gets the blood circulating and takes your mind off your worries will do. If physical activity is not recommended for health reasons, then knitting, baking, Sudoku, or the Sunday crossword can be your go-to activities.

Finding Your Balance

The advertising world's notion of retirement as a stress-free utopia is a nice idea but not terribly realistic in this modern age, where there are so many external stress factors in life, whether from family, or friends, or economics, or health. So while living stress-free is a great notion, it is a very difficult factor to effectively achieve outside a monastery.

However, *if you can establish a balance*, such that your lifestyle can be handled to your satisfaction and bring you peace of mind, then happiness will be yours. Do what you want to do, achieve what you want to achieve, and if you still have a little free time to relax before the train leaves, you've unquestionably done a terrific job in planning and implementing your Third Journey.

Case Study: *Is it possible to think about your health too much?*

Sam had been a senior-level executive in an international oil company and had traveled the globe countless times. In fact, he always said that his office was thirty-five thousand feet above ground. He knew that adjusting to mandatory retirement after such an active career would be a bit of a jolt, so in many respects he thought he was prepared. But when his retirement day actually arrived, he was caught off guard by the degree of emptiness that he felt.

Not having given much prior thought to how he would spend his days, he started to obsess about his health, for want of anything else to do. Even though he had always been in good health, he began to spend more and more hours at the gym but never seemed satisfied with the result—his weight was never low enough, his stomach never flat enough.

Even a positive report from his annual physical did not reassure him. Sure, he might be in good health now, but how long could that last?

He eventually realized that obsessing about his health was actually taking over his life. With all the other important parts of his life in balance, it annoyed him that his health should be consuming considerable time and energy in his waking hours. He actually began to worry that worrying about his health could be a catalyst for ill health. It seemed bizarre to his logical mind, but it was a concern nonetheless.

He didn't seek professional help or even discuss it with his wife. He wanted to work through it independently, in the same way he had handled all other problems in his working life. He knew that he was getting older—a fact that was nonnegotiable in his mind-set. He also knew that his health really was pretty good, so he worked out that all he had to do to restore a sense of well-being was research ideas on the Internet for developing healthy aging habits and put them into practice.

Today, Sam has accepted that by living a more balanced life, he will, in all probability, live for a good many years to come and that while he will expire at some point, it won't be any time soon.

Top Ten Tips for Your Journey

1. You are responsible for the overall state of your health.
2. Someone is going to win the longevity lottery—it might as well be you.
3. Chemical dependencies, including alcohol, can mask your ability to self-detect problems.
4. Find out all you can about chronic inflammation.
5. Find an eating regimen that suits your psyche, your lifestyle, and your body.
6. Don't put off checkups and things that don't seem right to you about your body.
7. The mind is a terrible thing to waste; use yours every day.
8. Your body *will* slow down as you age, so do things slower, but still do them.
9. Adjust your lifestyle and enjoy your new style of life.
10. Think young, but act your age.

CHAPTER 4

Overcoming the Fear of Change

The need to be constantly coping with change—positive change or negative change—is the most unexpected aspect of the Third Journey, yet it is our ability to adapt and morph as we age that either limits us or frees us up to live a long and happy life. In this chapter we will address the importance of overcoming the fear of change to migrate toward a new life of passion and vitality.

The hardest part to come to terms with, for many people, is that even positive changes can seem so unfair at first.

You work all your life on the premise that you will enjoy sunny, sleepy afternoons in a two-story house with a white picket fence, only to discover that your knees ache too much to weed the garden, and the water heater has sprung a leak and flooded the basement, and you don't have the money to replace the carpet.

You plan for a life of leisure, only to find you have no interest in being idle the moment you arrive in retirement. You look forward to the thought of Sunday afternoons with grandchildren, only to find they are completely immersed in after-school sports. You plan to spend your golden years with your loved one, only to have him or her pass away, leaving you to spend twenty-plus years on your own when you don't even know how you will make it to the end of the week.

Even if you know yourself, and you are a good planner, and your initial days at home are blissful, you will quite likely discover that *staying happy throughout* the Third Journey can be a daunting task.

DON'T RETIRE
REPURPOSE YOURSELF
AND
ENJOY THE JOURNEY

When you worked, you craved peace and quiet, and now you are ready to cry or scream if you don't find someone intelligent to talk to. You thought the person sitting across the breakfast table or a friend or relative would fulfill this need, only to discover that you have little in common with that person. You do your best to compensate by keeping busy, but there are so many hours in the day to fill, and your new habit of sleeping less just makes it even more difficult.

And then it hits you—how did you get stuck here anyway? Once upon a time, the young you had dreams. You were going to go to so many places and do great things. Whatever happened to all that energy and enthusiasm? *Whatever happened to your passion in life?*

Did it fall by the wayside as family obligations took priority?

Did you give up in frustration when the mountain became too steep to climb?

Or is your true purpose still lying dormant inside you, waiting to be discovered?

"What do you mean, true purpose? That sounds like a bunch of New Age mumbo jumbo!"

"Not at all. When you were in the work world, you had a purpose.

You were a banker, or a litigator, or a janitor, or a parent, or a pilot. But this was your work purpose."

"It was?"

"But now you don't do those things anymore, and you are adrift. In short, you need to repurpose yourself."

"Let me see if I get this—I worked forty years to get free, and *now* you are telling me that I have to get back to work?"

"Not necessarily *work*, per se, but you do need to identify and accept a new purpose to feel fulfilled."

The problem is that the things that we assumed we were going to do to fill the day in retirement are seldom sustainable in the long run. During your first year or so in the postwork world, most people tend to be happy as long as they are busy. The identifying of things to do and filling the day can itself be sufficient to keep a new Oldster occupied, but sooner or later most people find these activities lose their appeal—through boredom, injury, or the loss of suitable people to accompany them. We would like to be stimulated and challenged and entertained and find a way to give back to the community. Similarly, we need to steer clear of anything so strenuous and time-consuming that we become overwhelmed.

The idea of a job often gets consideration at a time like this. It does not necessarily have to be a paid position, but we need to feel appreciated and valued if we are giving our time and skill sets. Unless we actually need the cash (in which case, we will accept any position we can find), we tend to be a lot pickier regarding what we will take on; many of us have not yet reached the level of humility and simplicity required to view the task of being a professional greeter at the local big-box store or a tourist bureau as a self-fulfilling honor. Likewise, we are tempted to resent the endless hours of unpaid child-rearing that we provide to our grandchildren instead of appreciating the role that we play in shaping their core values and self-esteem.

This new journey can be equally if not more exciting than those years when you felt your employer needed you and that you were a critical component of his or her success. The Third Journey is your time and your choices. Those choices may impact many people, but most important, they matter to you and your well-being and retirement happiness.

Resisting Change

It is quite normal to stubbornly refuse to make any changes at first. It is possible that you will *not* move, or downsize, or install grab bars in the bathroom. You will *not* find new friends, or join a club, or go to church. The idea of facing strange new people is way too scary. You like things just as they are, thank you very much. The world and everyone in it can just go to blazes!

And the really tricky thing is that this sort of thinking actually works for a while. You build up a little head of steam, fuel it with a little indignation, and next thing you know, *you* are the cranky old person muttering to himself in the pharmacy that everyone whispers about.

The choice is yours. You can stay just as you are and be miserable forever, or you can make some changes.

In some ways, the people who have to make changes for financial reasons are the lucky ones (assuming they can still afford to keep a roof over their heads once they are done). They are pushed from their cozy complacency into brand-new situations and forced to try new things. It is, ironically, a lot harder for those of us in better financial circumstances to make changes because these changes *appear* to be optional.

"What do you mean, *appear?*"

"Simply that by this point in life, we are very good at making excuses and finding the easy way out. We have had sixty years to teach ourselves how to tailor our decisions to avoid facing up to our problems."

"And what, pray tell, is wrong with that?"

"Nothing, if you want to wind up living in one room of your house with a leaking roof and mold on the walls."

"What?"

"Let me put it this way. What happens to overweight people who continue to eat cupcakes and fried food?"

"They get fat and sick and put their lives in jeopardy."

"And why do they do this?"

"Because they don't care enough about what happens to them, and they are too weak to make any changes."

The terrible truth is that every time we have a problem, and we tell ourselves that we don't need to make any changes, we are just fooling ourselves.

This is not news. It is just that when we were young, this sort of behavior usually resulted in lost job opportunities, shopping addictions, or bad credit. Now that we are older, our bad decisions can put our lives in jeopardy. If you doubt this, consider the huge number of elderly people who have fallen on the stairs and broken a hip because they refused to move to a single-story house.

The evidence is clear—we must learn to adapt, or we risk the potential for catastrophic consequences.

So let's take a look at some of the things that typically prevent us from making changes and discuss a few ideas regarding how to overcome them.[17]

Holding Yourself Back

In some respects, the word "complacency"[18] is a strange word to be in a book about retirement and living the Third Journey. What is there to be complacent about? The reality, however, is that there are many aspects of our older years where some form of complacency holds us back.

"He's too set in his ways."

How many times have you heard that? More to the point, how many times have you understood it? What does it really mean? Most people take it to mean that he or she is stubborn, awkward, and simply refuses to budge—whether that's about an opinion or what he wants to watch on TV or eat for dinner. A grumpy old man, perhaps.

If even reading about the notion of making changes has you gritting your teeth, perhaps you might ask yourself the following questions:

17. If you are happily divesting yourself of everything that has been cluttering up your life and making plans to move to Goa, donate this book to someone in need now, and move on. Otherwise, hang in there. Help is coming.
18. Complacency is defined as "a feeling of quiet pleasure or security, often while unaware of some potential danger, defect, or the like."

- What is the payoff to not making any changes?
- Why does the idea of change make you so uncomfortable?
- Have you always been this way?
- Was there a significant event in your past that made you resistant to change?
- Are the reasons for initially rejecting the idea of change still valid?
- Is it still the best strategy for you to reject changes of any sort?
- Are there any small things that you could consider implementing to bring a little more balance to your thought and decision-making processes?

Thinking about the answers to these questions may not inspire you to rethink your position, but it is always good to understand why you behave the way that you do in stressful circumstances.

Fear of Fear Is the Only Fear

Having done certain things a certain way all your life, the idea that some big change is forced on you, regardless of how much time you have to think it over, is a disturbing issue for many people. As we age, our fear of the unknown increases. We become less stable, less at peace, and can envisage our health being impacted—in some cases, badly.

There is a sense of trepidation, where the effort to do something different can be a challenge, and we simply prefer to stay the way we are today. This is not a matter of being stubborn; rather, it's a concern that something new will cause us to feel upset. In other words, if we don't like being upset, why would we agree to a new idea?

We can easily get stressed out by having to adapt, learn, or change to someone else's way of doing things. We become anxious about having to move home, go into hospital, refinance our house, or make a long journey. It's the uncertainty of something new or different—the fear of the unknown. This may seem hard to believe at the fearless age of sixty-six, but older folks can build up a fear of change for days and weeks ahead of time, causing them to not sleep properly, not eat properly, and be irritable with everyone. All this trauma can lead to high levels of insecurity and a loss of self-worth.

In many cases, an independent professional advisor will recommend the change you need to make. If your doctor says that you must change your eating habits, drinking habits, or smoking habits, then maybe you should consider those changes. If your financial advisor suggests that you should change your spending habits or tighten your belt because your money won't last, then maybe you should make these changes.

Part of the underlying anxiety is not always the change itself but simply the *worry* that if this new thing doesn't work out, we may not have the emotional or physical stamina to face trying again, and we will get stuck in a dark, unhappy place. We also fear losing the time that it will take to make the adjustments—time that we will never get back.

Choosing to Change

Winston Churchill once said, "A change is as good as a rest."

Perhaps, but it depends on the circumstances.

A *forced* change is different from a *chosen* change, and the consequences can make you very upset or very happy. So why would we deliberately seek a change?

The change, especially if it is through choice, can easily be softened by endless preparation, not only in the physical or material changes but by getting psyched up for the new circumstances ahead of time. Get a picture in your mind of your new surroundings, for example, and create a video in the mind. Then play it time and time again, over and over. It will be surprising how many new angles you will discover in the replays. So by the time the big move occurs, you will have worked out all the nuances of the new situation.

If you are teetering on the edge of a decision, the first step is to acknowledge and accept that there is high probability that this change will cause you some (if not considerable) anxiety. Being ready for the stress is a safe way to handle the issue when it does come along. Make every effort to stay calm. There will be tough moments and easier moments; accept them both, and enjoy as many as you can.

Next, cut the task of changing something into bite-size bits. This applies to cleaning out the garage as much as it does to moving to Australia. The thing that stops people faster than anything is being overwhelmed

WILLIAM R. STORIE AND ROBIN W. TRIMINGHAM

by the sheer size of the task itself. Simply committing to working on whatever it is that needs to be changed for at least an hour a day until the task is accomplished will keep you focused on moving forward, rather than overthinking or overcomplicating the difficulty of the job. You can use this approach to do anything from losing weight, to cutting back on expenses, to trimming all the hedges in your garden, to painting the entire house.

The Price of Change

Another inhibitor to change is often the prohibitive perceived cost of making the change. Yes, you are on a fixed budget, but there is a way to raise the cash to do just about anything you set your mind to do. It is time to *push your ego aside* and employ a little creativity.

- So what if you have never repaired a toilet? What can you possibly do to it that a plumber could not fix if your efforts are unsuccessful?
- So what if you have never changed a kitchen faucet? If you can figure out how to turn off the water, you can wrestle the old tap off and take it to the hardware store to purchase a suitable replacement.
- So what if you have never grown vegetables? You can learn how to plant a garden on YouTube.
- So what if you have never shopped at a thrift store? Wear a hat—no one will recognize you (and if you do see someone you know, you will quickly discover that all that person wants to do is discuss the great bargains!).
- So what if you have never had a yard sale? You can get rid of all your junk and make enough money in one day to get the car repaired, or buy a plane ticket, or purchase craft supplies to make things to sell.
- So what if you have never clipped coupons? If you found a ten-dollar bill on the front porch, you would pick it up, wouldn't you? Well, guess what? In many areas, more than twice that amount is delivered in newspaper coupons every week.

- So what if you have always bought name-brand cleaning supplies? The no-name ones work just as well, and baking soda and vinegar are even cheaper and clean a great number of things without harsh chemicals that can harm the environment.

Okay, you get the point. Now walk around the house and start making a list of simple ways to save money, and if you are really stuck, just Google "money-saving ideas," and millions of suggestions will appear.

Family Challenges

Sometimes the most difficult inhibitor to change is external pressure exerted by family members. Most of the time the pressure to make changes is well intentioned and correct. The problem is that the idea of our child, an inexperienced forty-year-old, telling us what to do is intolerable. We are the grown-ups here, thank you very much. We are much more mature and experienced. We are not going to be told what to do by a mere child, and "that's final, young lady."

Except ... the youngster happens to be right, and we have now backed ourselves into a corner out of pride and will most likely be stuck there until we are ready to come out and say we are sorry.

Hmm. Perhaps it wouldn't kill us to let our children install grab rails in the bathtub or help us sort out the attic or mow the lawn.

Enough. If you are in this sort of a predicament, do something to get out of it. That meddling "kid" you find so objectionable just loves you and wants you to be safe and comfortable. Get over yourself, and let him or her help you out a little. It will make you both feel better, and you can still be a tad defiant when no one is looking now and again.

If, on the other hand, you are dealing with relatives who are trying to force you to make changes (or to prevent you from making changes) *for their own personal gain*, get help now. Put the book down, and call social services or legal aid, and get some expert help.

If what is happening to you is endangering your health, your safety, your life, or your financial security, you must take action. You have legal rights that must be respected, even if you are disabled or terminally ill.

Don't ever let anyone mistreat you because you are too embarrassed to admit you got fooled.

As you progress through your Third Journey, you will quickly discover that the only constant is change itself. Just as each year of childhood brought new opportunities and skills for you to master, such as learning to walk, tie your shoelaces, ride a bike, or drive a car, so too your Olderhood years will have skills for you to master and milestones to mark. What are you going to do to change your life for the better today?

Top Ten Tips for Your Journey

1. Use your mind to reenergize your body.
2. Everyone has problems at some point in life; you are not unique.
3. Change is challenging—forced or by choice; recognize that.
4. Handle change in small, manageable steps, not one big leap.
5. Fully understand all the costs involved in a change.
6. Old habits die hard; refresh them and start again.
7. Don't worry about lost time; you have a long journey ahead of you.
8. Don't let others make changes for you.
9. Take your time to make big-change decisions.
10. Think young, but act your age.

CHAPTER 5

Managing the Hard and Soft Impacts of the Aging Process

Age is a question of mind over matter. If
you don't mind, it doesn't matter.
—Leroy "Satchel" Paige

Sometimes when you are passing through unfamiliar territory it can be a little difficult to stay positive and optimistic regarding what the future holds for you. This is particularly true during the aging process because the journey requires us to manage and adjust to loss—the loss of mobility and independence, the loss of a home and the lifestyle that went with it, or the loss of a loved one.

This chapter discusses the effects of change in the Third Journey and the psychological consequences during the aging process. It is a collection of the treacherous places where Oldsters frequently break down. Use this chapter to better understand the challenges a loved one is facing or to conduct private self-analysis. Never be ashamed or embarrassed to seek professional advice regarding any of the challenges that emerge as you age. Health care and social service professionals have already heard every conceivable story, and it is unlikely that your situation will even faze them. There is *no* reason to suffer in silence when help is readily available.

As you read through this section, keep in mind that an event can have a hard impact or soft impact on a retiree's life. If that event is classified as a negative issue,[19] we call the real consequences of the event itself the *hard impact* and the underlying psychological consequences the *soft impact*. The differentiation between the two is not as obvious as it might appear. There is usually a clear understanding of the former, yet often a confused or perhaps fuzzy understanding of the latter.

For example, if a younger person is diagnosed with a chronic illness, then apart from the physical effect of the illness (hard impact), the person will inevitably experience a mixture of fear, sadness, stress, anxiety, or even depression (soft impact). Conversely, if the chronic illness is diagnosed in an older person, the situation becomes more complex. As we age, we are aware that illness will likely become more prevalent and perhaps more severe, but this awareness does not mean that we will manage it very well if or when it appears. The onset of the illness creates fear of time left and whether some of the dreams of retirement will be accomplished. The possibility of not seeing grandchildren grow up, for example, can cause high levels of anxiety and despair.

Depending on the severity of the issue, be it medical or financial, the physical aspects of the crisis are soon merged with the psychological, or soft, aspects. In other words, the worry factor creeps in, and various other consequences can appear—losing sleep, not eating properly, being constantly stressed, being snappish with the family, being angry with the medical professionals helping you, shortened attention span, and a general lack of interest in most things. In fact, it can be argued that the resolution of the physical issues may be hindered by the psychological issues taking control—taking over, in other words. A clear correlation between the hard and soft impacts is widely recognized. The more severe the issue, the closer the correlation.

In many cases of chronic illness, the focus by medical professionals is almost exclusively on the physical attributes (treatment, medicines, and so forth); that is, the hard issues. In other words, their primary concern is the patient and getting him better from a medical perspective. While the family is equally concerned about the medical treatments, they have another issue to contend with, over and above the psychological effect on the patient, and that's the psychological effect on the family themselves. To

---

19. A negative issue can be family, finance, or health related.

further complicate matters, while there are plenty of resources available to address the psychological needs of the patient, the family is usually left to cope for themselves without assistance, unless they seek independent counseling, which is often both expensive and time-consuming.

As a rule, society tends to directly associate a medical crisis with medical resolutions and the physical effect on the patient, but quite often it disregards the emotional or psychological impact on the patient. Clearly, the professional health care experts, in this example, will be fully conversant with the psychological impact, but they frequently downplay or disregard it because it does not fall directly within their area of expertise. This leaves family members struggling to understand the effect that the illness is having on their loved one (either through ignorance or because the patient hides his true feelings). Consequently, the family's ability to care for the patient adequately can be compromised.

Ironically, in today's world of medical solutions and access to health care and insurance, the hard impact is much more solvable than ever before, but the soft impact can be much more acute and more directly related to the negative issue than we perhaps realize.

While physical pain and suffering is most unwelcome in a person's life, it can be effectively managed with treatment and medication in most cases. However, the psychological pain and suffering may be deeper, longer lasting, and negatively impact the patient's will to live.

The onset of apathy can be equally debilitating as we age. The sense that there is nothing significant left to live for can become reason enough to stop trying. "I've lived to this age, and now this has happened. I've had good innings, so why get too excited about treatment and cure?"

The feeling of despair is all too common in the mind-set of the elderly. It is perfectly understandable, of course, but if there is a fair chance of full or even partial recovery, then medical professionals, family, and friends should make every effort to encourage the patient to stick at it. Until the patient truly believes that there is a reason that she needs to keep living, it can be extremely difficult, if not impossible, to persuade her that it is worth the trouble of fighting to keep going. Call it stubbornness, but unless you experience the trauma yourself, the concept of despair can be difficult for onlookers to comprehend.

The onset of anxiety and stress can escalate rapidly from mild depression to despair and even dementia. The older we get, the less able we seem to be to control, slow down, or even stop the downhill slide from one stage to the next. Perhaps due to less confidence in our recovery potential, or decreased financial capability to pay for help, or just reaching the giving-up stage, we don't treat the issue satisfactorily. In some cases, of course, we may not even recognize the impact that prolonged depression has on our well-being—or worse, we do recognize it, but we have reached the point where we no longer care.

The following list is a summary of the most common challenges facing Oldsters today. If you recognize the symptoms or patterns of behavior in any of these sections in you or a family member, try to have a conversation regarding this, or seek professional assistance:

Health

In any survey or clinical study, the primary concern of older people is their health. Regardless of their financial condition, lifestyle, location, or family circumstances, if a person does not enjoy good health, then other issues, serious or not, will always take a lower priority in his or her life.

"People are living longer than ever before. Many seniors live active and healthy lives. But there's no getting around one thing: as we age, our bodies and minds change. There are things you can do to stay healthy and active as you age. It is important to understand what to expect. Some changes may just be part of normal aging, while others may be a warning sign of a medical problem."[20]

Also, different types of illness affect people in different ways. That vague pain in your side might just be indigestion, or it might be something more serious. You can spend your days worrying about it because you fear what the diagnosis might be, or you can go for an ultrasound and get it checked out. Knowledge is power when it comes to managing your

---

20. "Seniors Health," MedlinePlus, US National Library of Medicine, accessed September 1, 2016, medlineplus.gov/seniorshealth.html.

health. It is far cheaper and less invasive to treat a small problem than it is to let it develop into something more serious. The most effective way to enjoy a long and productive Third Journey is to commit to understanding and maintaining your state of health.

Chronic Illness

The main chronic illnesses[21] in seniors include cardiovascular problems, cancers (various types), diabetes, arthritis, osteoporosis, asthma, and breathing difficulty.[22]

Any one of these illnesses creates a serious trauma in a person's life. The health issues can usually be addressed with a regimen of treatment and medication, but during that period of treatment and afterward, the worries and concerns of the patient and family are heavy. Carrying the medical burden is only part of the situation; the emotional trauma is significant and may have an equally long-lasting impact on the patient. This is a situation that "takes a village" to support the person who is afflicted—both to assist the person in managing his or her condition and to help the person lead as full and productive a life as possible.

At all times, the focus needs to be on a series of small goals that can be accomplished, not on the patient's limitations.

- Accept that everyone with a chronic illness is going to have good days and bad days.
- Pace yourself at all times, whether you are the patient or the caregiver.
- Continually ask your medical team to explain things to give you peace of mind.
- Create things to look forward to; this will help you stay positive.
- Keep in mind that it is possible to live a long time with many chronic illnesses.

21. Chronic illness is defined as an illness that is prolonged in duration and is rarely cured completely. While some chronic diseases contribute largely to premature death, others contribute more to disability. Centre for Chronic Disease Prevention, accessed October 6, 2016, http://www.ccdp.jcu.edu.au/our-research.
22. Ibid.

- Live in the moment every day.
- Do not let your illness discourage you from setting new goals and going after them.

Geriatric Conditions

Unlike a chronic illness, a geriatric illness may not cause severe physical pain or premature death. However, the existence of a degenerative geriatric condition can most definitely cause extreme discomfort and lead to many forms of depression.

The main types of geriatric illness are the following:

- delirium (a kind of temporary confusion)
- dementia (an illness, such as Alzheimer's disease, characterized by ongoing confusion and memory loss)
- urinary incontinence (or bladder problems)
- dizziness or a tendency to fall
- vision and hearing problems[23]

In many cases, the onset of a permanent geriatric condition can bring about worry, fear, and even panic, which can accelerate over time. As the illness progresses, so too does the emotional stress and despair. Talking to your family doctor or geriatric specialist regarding your prognosis has the potential to give you peace of mind. If you have the strength of character to accept the true facts of your situation, you can differentiate between what is worth worrying about and what is simply your own imagined fear.

Money

While health events are obvious—they clearly cause concern and typically cannot be hidden from friends and family—there are many

---

23. "Many Older Adults Have Both Chronic Illnesses and 'Geriatric Syndromes,'" American Geriatrics Society's Health in Aging Foundation, accessed October 6, 2016, http://www.healthinaging.org/resources/resource:many-older-adults-have-both-chronic-illnesses-and-geriatric-syndromes.

other traumatic events in a retiree's life that can cause equal concern. A financial collapse, for example, whether it is due to poor planning, economic downturn, improper investment management, or theft (the hard impact), can cause a variety of soft impacts, including immense hardship, worry, depression, anxiety, or anger. Yet the control of a person's money is usually a very personal thing, and as such, the confessing of problems can be withheld for a long time, even years. Embarrassment at how poorly a person has managed his money, compounded by pride, shame, guilt, and panic, make it likely that the person will avoid seeking assistance for extended periods, opting instead to suffer in silence.

The dilemma of deciding whether to pay the rent this month or afford an ever increasing regime of prescriptions is all too real for many older people. According to the OECD (Europe), on average, "13.5% of over 65s in OECD countries live in income poverty, defined as an income below half the national median. Poverty rates are higher for older people than for the population as a whole, which averages 10.6%."[24]

Clearly, as the economic turbulence of recent years takes its toll on pensions, savings, investments, and retirement income, this dilemma has increased dramatically. The retiree rarely has the ability to recoup financial loss to make up for the shortfall. Thus, when the unexpected expense pops up, the squeeze is severely felt. The choice can, in many instances, be simplified to buying A or B—but not both.

In fact, it can even be argued that due to an inability to create or otherwise get more money, the resultant frustration and panic can actually be the underlying catalyst for a deterioration of health.

For the vast majority of seniors, there are only three sources of income in retirement: (1) personal/company pension; (2) state pension; or (3) investment income. Obviously, a senior can seek part-time income as a source of extra cash, but the sustainability of that income depends on a person being in sufficiently good health to work regularly.

Therefore, any change or downward swing in retirement income will cause considerable stress for the senior. If there is little likelihood

---

24. "Pensions at a Glance 2011: Retirement-income Systems in OECD and G20 Countries," OECD, last modified 2011, https://www.oecd.org/els/public-pensions/47384613.pdf.

of the income levels being rebalanced, then there is a temptation to give in to despair instead of accepting responsibility for the situation and brainstorming ways to alleviate it.

This sort of situation is far easier to manage if retirement financial planning has been conducted properly, and a contingency fund has been established well in advance.

If, however, such planning was absent or minimal, then the ability to predict such income changes and to do something about it in advance or even in real time may be severely limited. On the other hand, if no prediction or an inkling of a downward swing was evident in advance, then the suddenness of any change will cause irreparable damage, not only to the person's bank account but also to her overall lifestyle and emotional well-being.

The other twist to poor planning is actually self-inflicted in many cases. Many people actually deny that they don't have enough money for adequate retirement, either through laziness, incompetence, or embarrassment to confess to friends and family. Many people simply choose to delay the calculations because the rainy day may never come. It *will* come, and if the planning has been ignored, then the rain turns into a downpour that may not be easily turned off. And even if they manage to dodge and weave their way to the end of their lives without incident, the spouse they leave behind is often saddled with a financial collapse at the moment they are least equipped to deal with it.

How much better it would be to seek advice while there is still time to make changes and balance your monthly budget. Yes, you may have to move or take in a tenant, but this is a small price to pay for maintaining your self-respect and independence.

Mortality

Within the aging process, people think about death—perhaps not every day and perhaps not very deeply, but they do think about it. As we age, the notion that we are getting closer to the end increases. That is perfectly normal and understandable. Sooner or later, everyone faces the reality of death. No one avoids it. Even so, some people simply ignore the issue and take life day by day as it comes along.

For many retirees, however, it is quite reasonable to not think about death very much until they have a clear and present reason to do so, and then it can become very difficult to think of anything else. For example, if a person has been diagnosed with a terminal illness, then the remaining days are numbered, at least to some degree, and it becomes necessary to decide fairly quickly whether to make the most of the time remaining or give in to despair.

No one wants to die, but given the inevitability of death, the admirable yet pragmatic approach is to lay the issue to the side, and get on with life. Even a terminal diagnosis that comes with an estimate of the amount of time left is just that—an estimate. There is no guarantee that you will fare better or worse than those who have gone before you, so you might as well go on living as though you have every chance of beating the odds, whether you have a day left, or a month, or twenty years. Get on with it, and do what you want to do. Enjoy those times fully.

The other side of the fear syndrome is finding the will to live and either defeating the illness or prolonging life through determination and willpower. While the fear issue will rarely disappear totally, many people seem to have the inner strength to combat seemingly huge medical and psychological obstacles when they have *a reason to keep living* that makes sense to them.

Contrary to what you might expect, it is quite possible to make peace with your circumstances and even accept that your time here is coming to a close, to the point that you don't think about it every waking moment. Studies indicate that this is easier for older people who have lived a full life than for someone in his or her early fifties. In fact, in many cases, the feeling that it's time to go may even start to surface in the back of their minds. This may be difficult for the younger reader to comprehend or accept, but the need for immortality in a person's youth frequently runs out of steam as the years move along.

Some people do experience extreme anxiety over the prospect of dying in their early retirement years when they are in perfectly good health. It would be inappropriate to say "ignore the issue," but it may be appropriate to at least suggest that you make more effort to live your life today, and don't be afraid to seek professional advice if you cannot put this fear to rest.

For many elderly people, then, the *fear of death* is less of a concern than the *fear of the unknown* or *the fear of losing control*. As we age, statistics show that our acceptance of death, albeit it at a date uncertain, becomes easier to reconcile in our minds. We find inner peace with the inevitable, and by doing so, the chances are that we are much more serene with the aging/dying process than ever we imagined. Obviously, our families may have their own separate issues and fears, which is understandable, and they have to deal with the situation in their own way, but if you can find that inner peace, the ending part of the journey may not be as bumpy a ride, psychologically, as first believed.

Other Things to Think About

Some older people are stubborn and simply don't want to be fussed over, wishing only to be left alone to "go in peace," but this does not mean that they should be left in isolation to fend for themselves. Every effort should still be made to attend to and comfort them.

In certain cultures and countries, the family gathers around the older members and tends to their needs in a pleasant and comforting fashion.

All things being equal, people typically get more comfortable with the thought of dying as they age. This is due to a number of factors:

- They have had more life experience.
- They are more content with what they have achieved.
- They have loved and been loved.
- They have made their peace with the fact that there is a limit to even the longest journey.
- Dying is an inevitable event.

Surviving Loss

The process of adjusting to widowhood/widowerhood after the death of a spouse or life partner can be as complicated and have as many stages as the illness that took the person from your life.

If someone in your household is critically ill, you need to prepare yourself for the inevitable (in this case, the *very* hard impact) in the best way you can. This can be very difficult, because at the end of life the patient frequently needs round-the-clock attention, and the primary caregivers miss meals and go for extended periods without sleep. Life becomes so completely about the patient that you just don't think about yourself or what life will be like afterward.

If your life partner passes suddenly, the shock can leave you numb for a period of time before the reality of the loss begins to surface.

In either case, if you did not have the opportunity to adequately prepare for this sad event, sorrow, fear, remorse, relief, guilt, and anger can swill around inside you, surging and ebbing without warning—the soft impact. One minute you may be coping, and then his or her coffee mug catches your eye, and you dissolve into a puddle of tears for forty minutes. Sleep may overcome you for hours at a time, or it may be completely impossible at night for several weeks. Be patient with yourself. Simply getting dressed and going about your day will be enough of a challenge in the beginning.

People can tell you what you "should" be doing or feeling, but they have no idea how your grief feels to you. They can tell you that it takes a year to recover, and perhaps for them it did take a year. But this does not mean that your recovery will be the same—it may take you three months or three years to feel like yourself again. It is equally possible that you may never feel like your old self again, but in time, you hopefully will learn to create a new life for yourself.

The critical thing to realize in overcoming grief is that you are not going to start to feel better *until you decide you are ready.*

You will feel sorrowful and empty until you are ready to let go of some of the pain you are feeling. This is easy for some people and very hard for others. If you are clinging to the pain of a lost loved one, you might consider whether you are secretly afraid to let the pain go because it would mean that you are acknowledging that the person you are pining for is gone. If this is the case, try to realize that the person is never gone as long as you remember him. Try to allow yourself to remember a few of the good things about the person when you start getting upset.

As mentioned, we are not psychologists, so if our thoughts on this issue do not resonate with you, talk to someone you trust who is a good listener. Talking about what you are going through will help you release little bits of your anguish so that you can breathe a little easier and think a little more clearly.

We also suggest that you resist the urge to make really big decisions too quickly unless there are financial reasons that you must make immediate changes. In that case, you have no alternative, so make them. Do not procrastinate; it will just make things worse. You probably will not make perfect decisions in your present state of mind, so just do your best to solve your largest and most immediate problems. You can always make more changes or adjust those already made when you are feeling more yourself and have had more time to consider what your needs really are in your new life.

The emotional toll on your mental and probably your physical state cannot be dismissed or downplayed. The psychological impact on your inner self must never be underestimated. You must be prepared to recognize and eventually accept that your emotional well-being will take time to heal.

Dating in the Third Journey

Whether by choice, divorce, death, or simply because the opportunity to marry never presented itself, many people find themselves living on their own in the Third Journey[25]—the hard impact. While the idea of having a place to yourself might have been a thrill when you were twenty and just heading out in the world, many Oldsters find coming home to an empty house almost unbearable.—one of the soft impacts.

Not surprisingly, there is quite a temptation to "partner up" for economic reasons, companionship, and even romance in the sunset years.

The physical side of love (the intimacy and sex) may have dissipated a while back, yet studies and reports clearly suggest that women, in particular, who have been left on their own may crave some form of intimacy. That's not to say that a man on his own doesn't have the same

---

25. According to the Administration on Aging, US Department of Health and Human Services, 2011, 45 percent of Americans older than age sixty-five are divorced, separated, or widowed. "A Profile of Older Americans," AARP, accessed October 6, 2016, http://www.aarp.org/content/dam/aarp/livable-communities/learn/demographics/a-profile-of-older-americans-2011-aarp.pdf.

cravings, just that men seem to cope with it differently (not better, perhaps, but differently). More on that later.

It is probably fair to say that women on their own will have a greater tendency to seek a romantic relationship than men. Leaving aside any cultural or religious stigma about dating as a widow, a woman need only ask herself whether she is ready for the idea of a new partner in her life.

Part of the excitement is that for the last several years in her now-ended relationship, the spark may have disappeared, and therefore, the romantic notion of being courted all over again in these elder years is a great adventure for many women. Having a man take her out to dinner, bring flowers or chocolates, hold her chair, call her daily, or drive her in his car are all little jumps of the heart that women enjoy. These are some enjoyable soft impacts stemming from the initial event of loss.

The notion that a new relationship *may* lead to intimacy is a part of the thrill, but in the majority of cases, it is fair to say that the very idea of a physical encounter with a new person is as scary as it is exciting to older women (and there are lots who would quite literally prefer not to have to address the possibility at all, preferring some romantic cuddling).

Our advice?

If physical intimacy is possible, and you want to experience this, then wade in gently; the right partner will understand a woman's hesitations instinctively and be patient. You should never feel pressured to do more than you are ready to or move faster than you are ready to, simply because you have done this before. Equally, never let your personal fears stand in the way of experiencing something that you know in your heart you truly want to do.

Men left on their own, on the other hand, often initially seek a younger woman, but they quickly discover that the reality of finding a younger woman is considerably more wishful thinking than fact. Yes, some younger women do like older men, maybe even prefer older men, but the statistics don't support the notion that a "hunk" of seventy-two years old can easily snare a thirty-five-year-old. It happens, of course, but it is the exception rather than the rule.

One of the obvious reasons why the majority of men don't feel comfortable dating again is the physical side of the deal. There's no question that things like performance-enhancing prescription drugs have changed that perception, but a man can be even more insecure about the "required" performance issues associated with a new sexual relationship.

Wow, she looks good for her age. I wonder what she's like in bed. Believe it or not, that's not an uncommon thought in the mind of the teenage boy trapped within the body of a male Oldster. Then reality arises—or not, as the case may be—and a little voice creeps into the back of his mind. *Egad, what if she does want to … and I can't?*

Men are very conscious of performance. Erectile dysfunction is a serious matter—perhaps not so much from a health standpoint (although it may indicate other medical problems) but certainly from a libido or macho perspective. A man will usually feel very disappointed, if not gutted, by not being able to satisfy his new partner, mostly because he does not appreciate just how forgiving and understanding a mature loving woman is of these things. Some men brush it off as being one of those things, but most men don't. They genuinely believe that no woman worth having would want them if the women knew about their inability to perform, never stopping to consider that she most likely lived with such a scenario for many years during her last marriage and never gave it very much thought. This could loosely be referred to as a soft impact.

This, therefore, may be one of the reasons why many men are hesitant to play the dating game when they first find themselves on their own. Over time, however, they may decide that a companion relationship would be nice and that the sexual aspects can be largely overlooked as irrelevant. If both partners in the new relationship are unperturbed by a lack of sex, then the man will feel so much better, relieved perhaps, and can get on with enjoying his new love in every other aspect of their lifestyles.

Finally, while the opinions of your offspring are important and should be listened to, they don't have to be adhered to. This is *your* life, and if you, man or woman, feel comfortable and psychologically at peace with dating and perhaps living together with a new mate, then the fears and concerns of others should be held in perspective. It may actually make more sense to experiment with a new relationship before making any long-lasting commitments. The old notion that we grew up with, whereby it was not proper to live with someone until marriage, may turn out to be, at this age, the very best advice to give yourself. Both men and women in their sunset years typically are not desperate to be in a new relationship, but they may simply like the idea and so will let nature take its course in its own sweet time.

Ancillary Factors

Most of the psychological-impact factors that older people experience are generated internally or through family influences. External factors, if available, also can increase peace of mind, but they can adversely affect elderly people if they are unavailable. Social service programs are available to varying degrees in different countries. The following is an overview of what is typically available in urbanized areas of the Western world.

Social Services

Social services are defined as being the services generally available to senior citizens in their community, which are provided by government, charitable organizations, or volunteer groups. It should immediately be recognized that charities and volunteer groups typically provide a best-efforts service, and as such, any criticism of shortcomings should be significantly tempered.

In many communities, the provision of various social services can be the difference between life or death, and none more so than in the retirement community. If health services, for example, which may not otherwise be handled by the retiree's health insurance, were to be withdrawn or severely cut back, then the impact on the retiree would be immense, not only due to the loss of the medical attention but causing emotional stress. The well-being of many Oldsters is dependent on those services, and any loss would seriously affect their quality of life. Hospitals, clinics, care centers, refuge centers, prescription drug provision, and so forth are all important facilities.

Legal aid is another important function of a social services menu. Legal aid provides legal advice, either free of charge or at minimal cost. Many times, lack of money or fear of embarrassment can hold someone back from resolving an issue. People will not do anything but will hope that the issue will resolve itself. But this service gives seniors a chance to take charge and resolve those issues.

Financial assistance can also be a lifesaving facility for seniors. If the senior runs into financial difficulty and has no other means of support, through family or savings, then the ability to seek help from government agencies may be critical. It may be classified as the facility of last resort by many seniors and may also cause undue embarrassment, but if such assistance is available, then the emotional relief can make an enormous difference to the well-being of the senior. Assistance to meet the normal daily costs of food, housing, insurances, and utilities may be provided.

Most seniors will be determined to feed, clothe, and house themselves, whether through pride or simple determination, but when the ability to self-provide, for whatever reason, dissipates, then the community should be willing to stand up and help. The lack of assistance facilities through care homes, food banks, clothing charity shops, and so forth makes the lifestyle of the senior difficult, and the psychological trauma increases.

In many communities, government-funded transportation makes the difference in an Oldster's being able to move about the community. Many seniors do not have their own transportation, especially due to cost of maintaining a car that is seldom driven. As such, the withdrawal of free transports would have a major impact on the mobility of the senior, and the stuck-at-home syndrome would increase his or her stress level.

So the message for your Third Journey is straightforward.

These years are the years you have to live your life, to do the things you want to do, go the places you want to go, and be with the people you want to be with. Make it your mission to deal with the hard impacts of the events that you experience in an efficient, thoughtful manner. Don't ignore the third-party resources that are available all around you to deal with the soft impacts. The day will come when you can neither look backward nor forward, but for the time being, you should make every effort to enjoy the journey, and be at peace with yourself day by day.

It is not death that a man should fear, but he
should fear never beginning to live.
—Marcus Aurelius Antoninus (AD 121–180)

Top Ten Tips for Your Trip

1. Every effort should be made to stay positive.
2. Face up to your age number and accept its ramifications.
3. Don't ignore health signals; act soon.
4. Fear of the unknown can be overcome through knowledge.
5. Recognize your inner feelings and emotions.
6. Analyze and review your troubled thoughts.
7. Don't despair; share with family and friends.
8. Make the effort to seek new interests.
9. Be frugal on luxuries and rational about necessities.
10. Think young, but act your age.

HEALTH CONSIDERATIONS

CHAPTER 6

The Importance of Taking Control of Your Health

Tell me what you eat and I will tell you who you are.
—Jean Anthelme Brillat-Savarin

Although many people enjoy relatively good health up to the point that they retire, there is no denying that our bodies are aging and about to undergo a change in what is required to keep them in top condition. In this chapter we will discuss the importance of learning to take proper care of your health and adapting to the changing needs of your body as you age.

The marvel of the modern age is that medical advances have evolved to the point where there is literally a pill for everything. Have a headache? Take a pill. Got a fever—no worries; we've got you covered. How about a toenail fungus? No problem; just take a dose once a day for three months, and you're cured. If only it was that simple.

A Holistic Approach to Wellness

If people really require a special cream or potion for every little ailment, how did the human species survive prior to 1900? Granted, outbreaks of famine and disease were frequent throughout human history, but some people lived long and healthy lives despite their harsh and primitive circumstances. This would imply that the ability to "live long and prosper" must be at least a bit instinctive. If that is the case, what has become of our genetic ability to self-heal?

Okay, perhaps this is a bit of an extreme idea, but it is also not too difficult to argue that the huge advances in the fields of science and medicine have made people more complacent than ever before. Not that long ago, the very existence of the human species depended on the concept of the survival of the fittest, and everyone knew the importance of maintaining health. Now we more or less take it for granted that we can abuse our bodies and depend on medical science to patch us up.

As mentioned, we are not doctors, nutritionists, scientists, or psychiatrists. We are not discounting the good work that anyone involved in the health care industry does to save the lives of those who are sick, and we are *definitely not* suggesting that you should disregard the advice of your medical practitioner if you are undergoing any type of treatment. We do, however, believe in common sense (the sort your grandmother and great-grandmothers were full of). It is only common sense to realize and accept that in most instances, *you are completely responsible for the overall state of your health, whatever that may be.*

Rare genetic anomalies aside, this is true in regard to your current state of health and your *future* state of health. We are not suggesting that the world should revert to the Dark Ages before penicillin and disinfectant, but we are suggesting that the introduction of the bathroom pharmacy has encouraged people to reach for a pill to mask the symptoms when something hurts, instead of listening to their bodies to get at the root cause of the discomfort. More importantly, in its earliest stages, this root cause of discomfort is often something that can be alleviated or even cured by altering personal habits and behaviors. To clarify what we mean, think about what happens when you overeat at an all-you-can-eat buffet—your stomach expands, your clothes feel uncomfortably tight, and in extreme instances you might even develop gas, stomach cramps, a headache, or a bout of constipation. All these symptoms are your body grabbing you and calling out, *"Yo, genius! Just because it's an all-you-can-eat buffet does not mean that guacamole and sweet potato pie are a good mix! And don't even start me on the five desserts you just stuffed into me! What are you thinking?"*

Most of us know what we *should* do and what we *should* eat, but as we are in our second childhood, we seem to think that it is okay to rationalize not doing these things and then launching into a mixture of anger, denial, and self-pity when it turns out that our years of overeating, drinking, pill popping, and stubbornness actually damaged our bodies to the point that we are sick.

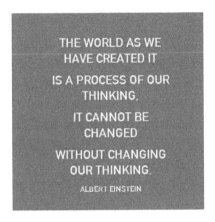

THE WORLD AS WE HAVE CREATED IT IS A PROCESS OF OUR THINKING.

IT CANNOT BE CHANGED WITHOUT CHANGING OUR THINKING.

ALBERT EINSTEIN

The problem with this sort of behavior is that while we might enjoy behaving like naughty children, our bodies are not kids anymore. Our cells are not the spring chickens they once were; it takes us longer to process the food we eat. Our energy levels have decreased, our circulatory systems are more sluggish, and it takes longer to recover from illness because we are not as strong as we once were.

Eventually, it all comes down to one simple decision: are we content to become a weak decrepit blob, fit for little more than watching television, or do we want to take proper care of ourselves and our loved ones and enjoy the freedom that we worked so hard to achieve?

If you want to enjoy an active, vital life, it is time to accept that the only way to stay healthy and strong enough to actually enjoy the Third Journey is to make a command decision to take control of your health and gradually work on it until it is in as good a state of repair as possible.

"Okay, command decision—check. Now what?"

"Well, do you know what the true condition of your overall health is now?"

"Average, I guess."

"You guess? How about you stop guessing and find out exactly what state you are in?"

Putting the Health Picture Together

Many factors go into putting together an accurate picture of your health. An obvious place to start is to go to the doctor for a checkup. Cooperate with any recommended tests, but don't be a passive observer to the process. Ask questions regarding the purpose of the tests. When you get the results, ask for a detailed explanation of their meaning in layman's terms. For example, ask what your blood pressure actually is and whether it is considered, high, low, or optimal for your age. Similarly, find out what your blood sugar level and cholesterol level are and whether or not they are within the normal range.

Listen to the benefits and side effects of all drugs prescribed, and ask what else you can do to improve your condition. Don't be complacent. Ask if there is any way to improve your health to the point that you don't need to take the prescribed medication. It is fine if this is not possible, but sometimes a new diet and exercise will work wonders.

Now that you have collected your starting data, you can do some other basic calculations that may or may not have been part of your physical, depending on where you live and the type of health insurance you have, that can provide insight regarding how much work you will have to do to significantly increase your life expectancy. For example, did you know that the number of hours you sit in a day is a key determining factor in predicting life expectancy?

Calculating Your Fitness Age

Scientists at the K. G. Jebsen Center of Exercise in Medicine at the Norwegian University of Science and Technology are conducting a worldwide study on the difference between chronological age (how old you actually are) and your fitness age (the maximum amount of oxygen you can take in while exercising).[26] Although determining your fitness age usually requires sophisticated laboratory equipment, you can get a good idea of what both your VO2 max and fitness age are by answering a few simple questions, such as your age, gender, waist size, height, and exercise habits, using a free online fitness age calculator

Be prepared if you decide to figure out your fitness age—you may not like the answer that you receive, but keep in mind that knowledge is power, and your number is just that—a number. Now that you know what it is, you can change it a little or a lot.

Researchers at the US Centers for Disease Control and Prevention have been working on a similar initiative and just released the results of the first study to provide population-level estimates of heart age nationwide. The report concludes that three out of four US adults have a predicted heart age that is older than their chronological age, meaning that they are at an increased risk for heart attacks and strokes. On average, men have a heart age eight years older than their chronological age, while women have a heart age five years older.[27] According to Barbara A. Bowman, PhD, director of CDC's Division for Heart Disease and Stroke Prevention, this is important because many adults "don't understand their

---

26. Fitness age is based on the concept of VO2 max, which is the maximum amount of oxygen you can take in while exercising. Your VO2 max can be used as a measure of cardiovascular endurance; if yours is below average compared to other people your age, it means your fitness age is actually greater than your chronological age.

On the other hand, a better-than-average VO2 max could mean your fitness age is younger than your age in years. Even better, it's possible to improve your VO2 max, which means your fitness age can actually get younger as you get older. "How Your Fitness Age Can Indicate Longevity," Dr. Mercola, last modified November 07, 2014, http://fitness.mercola.com/sites/fitness/archive/2014/11/07/how-fitness-age-indicate-longevity.aspx.

27. Heart age is the calculated age of a person's cardiovascular system, based on his or her risk factor profile. The risks include high blood pressure, cigarette smoking, diabetes status, and body mass index as an indicator for obesity. "Most Americans Hearts Are Older than Their Age," US Department of Health and Human Services, Centers for Disease Control and Prevention, last modified September 1, 2015, http://www.cdc.gov/media/releases/2015/p0901-heart-age.html.

cardiovascular disease risk; they are missing out on early opportunities to prevent future heart attacks or strokes."

Calculating Your Heart Age

You can calculate your heart age by using a free online calculator, which can be found easily by performing a Google search.

As with all things relating to your health, be sure to discuss these results with a medical professional before making any changes to your daily routine, and don't be disheartened if the prognosis seems daunting. It is never too late to start making changes, and there really are many simple things that you can do to improve your results. One study, for example, indicated that *just four minutes* of intensive exercise four times a week was sufficient to improve your VO2 max, so just think what a difference you could make by watching one less hour of television (or social media) for a day and going for a walk instead!

Calculating Your Body Mass Index

If you really want to take your fitness level seriously, you can also calculate your Body Mass Index (BMI), which is an assessment of your percentage of body fat, based on height and weight. The normal range is dependent upon your age and gender. The resulting measurement ranges include underweight, desirable (normal), overweight, and obese. Your BMI is important because excessive body fat makes you more susceptible to serious health conditions, including high blood pressure, heart disease, stroke, and diabetes. According to the Mayo Clinic, the top three things you can do to improve your BMI score include:

- *Embrace healthy eating* by choosing a variety of nutrient-rich foods, including fruits, vegetables, and whole grains and small amounts of energy-dense foods like olive oil, nuts, and dried fruits.
- *Exercise.* Aim for thirty to sixty minutes of moderately intense age-appropriate exercise daily.

- *Set action goals* focused on specific healthy activities, such as improving muscle tone through strength training or starting a daily food and activity diary.[28]

You can calculate your BMI manually using the following formula. If math is not your thing, there are also plenty of free online BMI calculators on the Internet.

	Calculate Your Body Mass Index (BMI)	Example
1	Multiply the weight in pounds by 0.45 (the metric conversion factor)	150 lb x 0.45 = 67.5
2	Multiply the height in inches by 0.025 (the metric conversion factor)	67" x 0.025 = 1.675
3	Square the answer from step 2	1.675 x 1.675 = 2.81
4	Divide the answer from step 1 by the answer from step 3	67.5 /2.81 = 23.42

The BMI of a person who is five foot seven and weighs 150 pounds is 23 and falls within the "desirable" weight category.

BMI Ranges	
Underweight	Less than 18.5
Desirable	18.5—24.9
Overweight	25.0—29.9
Obesity Class 1	30.0—34.9
Obesity Class 2	35.0—39.9
Obesity Class 3	More than 40

Embracing the Health Care Revolution

Up to this point we have talked extensively about the importance of diet and exercise as it relates to longevity. If we had written this book a few

---

28. "Weight Training: Improve Your Muscular Fitness," Mayo Clinic, last modified August 14, 2015, http://www.mayoclinic.org/healthy-lifestyle/fitness/in-depth/weight-training/art-20047116.

years ago, this is where we would have stopped, but advances in science and technology are reshaping our understanding of the human body on a daily basis and revolutionizing how we view illness and aging. It is important that you keep abreast of these changes.

Knowledge is your best defense when it comes to your long-term health and wellness. It is as important to keep learning about health care as it is to commit to becoming the master of your health. Everyone has heard the expression "your body is a temple." Try to embrace what this really means or at least be open to the idea that the fate of your health—and ultimately your longevity—is much more in your control than we were raised to believe. Granted, no one knows how long they ultimately will live, but there is nothing to stop you from adding years to your life by taking a few corrective measures now. We cannot stress strongly enough and often enough the importance of making a personal health and wellness plan with your chosen medical practitioner.

Top Ten Tips for Your Journey

1. You are in charge of your health; be responsible.
2. Always take your prescription medicines.
3. Know what you can eat; eat wisely.
4. Calculate your heart age.
5. Calculate your BMI.
6. Work out a light to moderate exercise routine—and do it.
7. Read up about inflammation and adopt your findings.
8. Remain active, physically and mentally.
9. Find your motivation to follow your life routine.
10. Think young, but act your age.

CHAPTER 7

The Interrelationship between Diet, Exercise, and Psychomotivation

It all comes of liking honey so much.
—Winnie the Pooh (A. A. Milne)

Now that we have unraveled our balls of twine and committed to living to be one hundred, let's swallow hard and have a frank chat about the thing we least want to discuss—our expanding waistlines. Health becomes an increasingly important factor for many people as they age. In our earlier years, the health-conscious among us paid attention to diet, fitness, fat content, and so forth, but unfortunately, many people did not pay attention to these issues. The famous words of Mickey Mantle—"If I had known I was going to live this long, I would have taken better care of myself"—take on an increasingly poignant meaning. In this chapter, we will explore the relationship between proper nutrition, fitness, and body fat.

The Importance of Proper Nutrition

When we were teenagers, all we had to do to lose weight was stop eating dessert, and the pounds melted away. Now, even though we eat and drink less and less of the things we love, we seem to have lost the ability to lose weight altogether. How can this possibly be?

Clearly, as we age, our minds and bodies change. What we did by way of exercising when we were thirty-five is not what we are able to do or even are willing to think about doing at age sixty-five. In our minds we may feel as though we have not aged, but the body says differently.

Having said this, the issue of diet, exercise, and overall fitness is not a one-size-fits-all matter. We all recognize that we have to adjust our physical activities as we get older. We don't have to eliminate them, and in fact, there is reason to suggest that, in some respects, the *more* we do, the better our overall well-being will become.

The simple truth is that for all the hype about the importance of nutrition, most of us don't really think that our diets are all that bad and wouldn't really know how to make healthier choices anyway. The first step to overcoming your dietary delusions is to take a good hard look at what you are actually putting in your mouth by staging your own personal "food intervention."

This can be much more difficult than you might expect because we are great rationalizers when it comes to analyzing our own diets. We don't count the three spoons of sugar we put in our coffee, we neglect to mention the candy bar that we ate in the car because we didn't have lunch that day, we consume an entire tub of ice cream and list it as one serving, and we tell ourselves that beer-battered fish and chips was close enough to grilled fish with broiled sweet potato that was listed on our meal plan.

We don't see these little omissions as self-sabotage of our future selves, so if possible, ask someone you live with to keep the list for you. There is nothing like being jolted back to reality by a complete list of your culinary sins to make you realize what you are doing to your body.

If you don't have anyone you can trust to assist with your food intervention, or if your dietary sabotage is aided and abetted by the food enabler[29] in your life, or if you are unwilling to expose yourself to possible scrutiny and embarrassment, you can download one of the many food apps off the Internet designed to help you manage your weight, and enter

---

29. Please note that definitions of a food enabler vary. It can be defined as any person who supports, condones, or assists someone who overeats. This may be a complex codependent relationship, requiring professional help to understand and resolve, and as such is beyond the scope of this book.

your food list there. This has the added benefit of allowing you to get a glimpse of the actual nutritional value (or lack thereof) of what you are feeding yourself.

Once you have created your food list, circle every item in red that contains fat, sugar, or alcohol, then try to try to come up with a lower-fat or lower-sugar alternative that you would still enjoy. As for alcohol, we will simply point out that each glass of rum and cola contains a combined total of seven teaspoons of sugar. If that doesn't seem like a lot to you, measure out seven spoons of sugar into a bowl and keep it on the kitchen table to remind yourself what you are about to consume each time you go for a refill.

It is time to swallow hard and face the fact that your body interprets everything that you put in your mouth as a chemical, and *the overall state of your health will largely depend upon the quality and the quantity of the food that you consume.*

What we are proposing here is not a diet plan; it is quite likely that you will lose a few pounds, but this is *not* the objective. *This is a permanent lifestyle change.*

Unless you know yourself to be an all-or-nothing personality type when it comes to making difficult changes, or your doctor recommends an immediate and radical change for health reasons,[30] you should not try to completely change your diet all at once unless you want to experience uncomfortable withdrawal symptoms and food cravings. Start by discussing a few small changes with a doctor or nutritionist, and once you have adjusted fully, take another look at your diet and see what else you can change.

The degree to which you will succeed in improving the overall state of your health literally depends on the extent to which you make permanent changes to the way you feed yourself. This means that simply eating a smaller portion of your existing diet is not the answer, even if you do manage to shed a few pounds, because cutting back on a greasy junk

---

30. As with anything related to your health, discuss your dietary strategy with a physician or qualified dietitian. If radical changes are prescribed, follow them faithfully. You can look online for support in discussion forums, or join a support group in your area to help you through the initial phase until you become more accustomed to your new way of eating.

food diet is not going to improve your ability to stay strong and fight off infection. Only highly nutritious food will do that.

Similarly, yo-yo dieting, in which you eat smaller portions of healthier food during an initial dieting phase and then resume eating larger portions once you have lost a few pounds, is rarely effective. You most likely will gain back some or all the weight because you are consuming more food—all the excess calories (albeit more nutritious ones) are converted into sugar by your body and stored as fat.

"Are you saying that there is no way to lose a significant amount of weight?"

"There are lots of ways to lose weight, but there is only one way to keep it off—make permanent changes to the quality of your food *and* your portion sizes, and learn to enjoy your new eating routine."

"But I like my current diet!"

"I am sure you do, but look at it this way: would you knowingly put bad gas in your car?"

"Of course not!"

"Would you overfill the gas tank so that the fuel spilled all over the ground?"

"No."

"Then why are you treating your car better than your body?"

If you're ready to take another swing at improving your diet, check out the components of the Mediterranean diet that we discussed in chapter 3. Then, keeping allergies or food intolerances in mind, search for a few new recipes online, or treat yourself to a new cookbook. Who knows? You might discover that vegetables taste different from the way that you remember them or at least discover a new cooking hobby.

The Fitness Roller Coaster

Now let's talk about the fitness roller coaster we all have been on for the last fifty years. The baby boomers were the world's first true fitness generation, and we have tried and purchased just about every conceivable fitness gadget known to man.

We were the generation that made aerobics sexy, for goodness sake! In our twenties and thirties, we bought entire Spandex wardrobes, complete with leg warmers and high-top sneakers, and wore them to the grocery store, just like Pat Benatar. We consumed gallons of frozen yogurt that we didn't even like and faithfully watched *The Twenty-Minute Workout* on television—and occasionally we even did some of the exercises ourselves.

We religiously watched exercise equipment infomercials for Ab Rollers, rowing machines, universal gyms, rebounders, Bowflex systems, and inversion boots (remember those?) and even purchased a few of them. We gave up smoking; switched to lite beer, diet cola, and low-fat toaster pastries; and still we weighed more than the average 1950s housewife. How can life be so unfair?

Okay. Time for a reality check.

The bad news is this: until a few years ago, medical and scientific research in our lifetime focused mainly on surgical and pharmacological means of extending life and more or less continued to assume (yes, *assume*) that an increase in physical activity would result in a loss in weight. If you doubt this, consider that most of the major life-extending scientific research and surgical procedures have been developed in our lifetime:

- 1922: Frederick Banting and Charles Best discover insulin.
- 1928: Alexander Fleming discovers penicillin.
- 1950: Gertrude Elion develops chemotherapy to treat leukemia.
- 1954: Doctors perform first successful kidney transplants.
- 1967: Christiaan Barnard carries out first human heart transplant.
- 1972: Geoffrey Hounsfield invents the CAT scanner
- 1980s: MRI scans are developed to monitor the electrical activity of the brain.

Amazingly, no one thought to study what the relationship between diet and exercise actually is. The widespread interest in fad diets and nutrition didn't even begin until the 1960s, when Jean Nidetch introduced the *Weight Watchers Cookbook*. Since that time, we have continued to be the generation most experimented on, to determine how our bodies respond to changes in fitness and diet in the hope of introducing a "quick fix" that will enable us to lose weight and keep it off.

The Relationship between Diet and Obesity

In a 2013 study released by researchers from Loyola University,[31] they set out to challenge the idea that exercise is an effective way to combat obesity. Ironically, when the study began, the researchers thought they would prove that exercise is a crucial component for weight loss, but "the science shows that the largest driver behind obesity is not how sedentary people are, but instead how poor their diet is." It turns out that the more people work out, the more their appetite increases. The problem with most popular diet advice is that it puts the importance of exercise on an equal par with calorie restriction, implying that if you exercise enough, you can pretty much eat whatever you like. This is simply not the case; only nutritious food and portion control will result in permanent weight loss.[32] Keep in mind that this new research should not be viewed as an excuse not to exercise—you need moderate exercise to maintain adequate lung function, muscle mass, and flexibility.

After reading this, if you still think it's okay to spend your postwork life as an armchair athlete with a doughnut in one hand and the TV remote in the other, consider the following: more than half the people in Australia over the age of seventy-five have some sort of chronic disability that makes it difficult for them to walk or maintain their independence. It is one thing to spend your days in an easy chair by choice, but how would you feel if your body weakened to the point that you could no longer get up, and you knew that this was something you *probably could have prevented?*

We are not suggesting that everyone will be able to climb Mount Everest on their eightieth birthdays, but the latest research now suggests that staying physically active can help to reduce or even reverse the risk

---

31. "Physical Activity Does Not Influence Obesity Risk: Time to Clarify the Public Message," Oxford Journals, Medicine & Health, *International Journal of Epidemiology* 42, no. 6, last modified July 13, 2003, http://ije.oxfordjournals.org/content/42/6/1831.
32. Ibid.

of many disabilities and chronic diseases because many factors associated with aging are exacerbated by *inactivity*.[33]

The Benefits of Staying Active

Now let's consider some of the benefits of staying active. Your muscles become weak when you don't exercise as a young person, and this process continues as you age, to the point that it can become difficult to support the weight of your own skeleton. This is compounded by the loss of bone density due to inactivity and poor diet and a loss of joint mobility, to the point that you can become unsteady on your feet and be seriously injured if you trip and fall.

Moreover, if you are injured and require surgery or physiotherapy, the stronger you are entering treatment, the stronger you will be coming out of it, and the easier it will be for you to get yourself up and moving again.

Walking, strength training, Tai Chi, yoga, water aerobics, and stretching are particularly beneficial for slowing the rate of bone loss, increasing muscle mass while reducing fat, and maintaining joint flexibility, balance, and coordination. Physical activity can also be a great way to spend time with other people and have a little fun. Research from Stanford University indicates that older people who walk regularly tend to have the least amount of brain shrinkage over time, and it can positively affect the hippocampus region of the brain, which is associated with memory.

The Third Journey is literally the move-it-or-lose-it phase of life. There is no doubt that by participating in regular age-appropriate exercise and consuming controlled portions of nutritious food you can keep yourself mobile and independent and even reverse some of the deterioration that has already taken place.

The question is, are you ready to employ a little self-discipline?

---

33. Osteoarthritis, osteoporosis, and rheumatoid arthritis are more common in older people. Exercise to increase muscle and bone fitness can reduce or reverse the risk of disability and disease. "Aging—Muscles Bones and Joints," Department of Health & Human Services, State Government of Victoria, Australia, last modified November 2012, https://www.betterhealth.vic.gov.au/health/conditionsandtreatments/ageing-muscles-bones-and-joints.

Psychomotivation and Health

In a broad sense, psychomotivation can be found in various different parts of our lives—our personal financial planning, family matters, meeting new people, and so forth—but none more so than in fitness, exercise, health, and nutrition.

Despite the fact that we could easily get off the couch and go to the gym, a lot of us Oldsters simply lack the motivation to do so. We can comprehend that by going to the gym and running on a treadmill, we will, over time, help our cardiovascular well-being, but we just don't see any reason to bother. Maybe we're complacent. Maybe we're embarrassed. Maybe we believe that we don't need to because we are already generally healthy, or our doctor has told us that we are considered healthy for our age, or we got this far without using a treadmill so why start now? Whatever the excuse, the underlying cause of our lethargy is simply that we have no real, tangible, or plausible reason to do otherwise.

So how do we handle this psychomotivation issue? We identify a specific reason to motivate us to make changes, and then we adjust our lives, our eating habits, our physical activity, and so on, *related* to that purpose to turn it into a reality.

It is too broad and too loose to simply say, "If I exercise, I will live longer," but identifying a specific goal, such as deciding that you want to see your grandchildren graduate college, get married, or have kids of their own, just might be reason enough to cause you to actually change your habits.

Perhaps, but no matter how good your intentions, you will battle your own inner rationalizer every step of the way.

Too many people these days are very conscious of health and fitness and diet, yet they justify their wine drinking, for example, by acknowledging that while they do watch what they eat, or go to Pilates, or get enough sleep, they feel that "at this age" they have earned the right to enjoy themselves a little. They could be right. Their metabolism may very easily cope with a variety of "abuses," and they may genuinely feel in good health—and that is perfectly fine if their coping mechanisms are in good shape. Unfortunately for many of us, though, we abuse our bodies, regardless of the known consequences. We rationalize behavior like this by saying that we enjoy living as we do, and we are at peace with our decision—a very dangerous state of denial indeed.

However, if you have or can find or even manufacture a solid, rational, and achievable purpose and support it with a path of realistic minigoals, then you may very well discover that better eating habits, more exercising, and closer attention to your body will amalgamate into a better lifestyle—now and for many years to come.

Motivate, activate, and appreciate.

Top Ten Tips for Your Journey

1. Watching the waist can be a waste of time—but try anyway.
2. There is no secret or magic pill to control your weight. You have to adopt a healthy lifestyle, and stick to it.
3. The better your reason for getting out of bed in the morning and taking care of your health, the more likely you are to do so.
4. If you eat to live, rather than live to eat, you may live longer.
5. Exercise is not a bad word.
6. Find an age you like, and stick with it; find an exercise you like, and stick with it.
7. You don't have to lift weights at the gym to increase muscle tone; lift the grandkids.
8. Establish your own personal reasons to watch your diet and exercise.
9. Remain active in mind and body, but get adequate sleep.
10. Think young, but act your age.

MONEY MATTERS

CHAPTER 8

The Psychological Consequences of Poor Financial Planning

Will I have enough money when I retire?

A lack of financial planning for retirement can have a significant impact on a person's well-being for the rest of his or her life.

The two fundamental issues are "How much money will I need?" and "How long will I live?"

The short answer to both questions is "Don't know."

Although the answers are fuzzy, that is no excuse for not trying to get a handle on the issue. To a great extent, the amount of money needed is related to what you intend on doing in the Third Journey. If you want to travel extensively, especially at the front of the plane, then your needs will be higher than if you choose to travel less often or prefer to purchase economy class. If you believe that in these latter years you deserve luxury and pampering, then fine—as long as you can pay for it in the short term and still have enough to see you through your later years, when you may not feel the same need to treat yourself quite as well as before.

So the balance between living the high life and the psychological feel-good factor is key. The notion that it is smart to spend money because you deserve it or to show family and friends that you intend to enjoy yourself, regardless of the cost, is foolhardy at best and financial suicide at worst. Financial planning is not something done for the front years of your retirement; it is done for *all* the years of your retirement.

In this chapter we will address the emotional or psychological factors associated with the critical need to make financial predictions for your retirement and then manage your retirement finances when you cross the threshold, while not losing sight of the potential fear of running out of money and that money concerns will affect every aspect of your Third Journey. In the following two chapters we will focus on preretirement financial planning, including the preparation of a budget, and then the postretirement adjusting and managing your finances.

So let's get started.

Retirement Spending Patterns

If you expect that your expenditures throughout your Third Journey will follow a fairly stable and predictable pattern, and if your asset base is focused on income generation rather than value-driven strategies (where regardless of how long you live, you will have a steady income stream throughout the rest of your life), then the only major obstacle would be an unexpected catastrophe in your life, such as a health matter, major repairs to your house, a family event requiring significant financial support, and so forth.

Typically, your asset base will consist of your workplace pension, your government pension, your investment income, and part-time income, if applicable. These sources of income combine to generate your overall retirement income.

Thus, leaving aside the unexpected event, if your income and expense budgets are in sync with each other, and you don't rashly decide to go on a huge spending spree, your psychological comfort level regarding your standard of living will be satisfactory. While you may not have much extra cash left at the end of each month, if you have stabilized your budget, you will be able to achieve financial peace of mind.

But if you failed to accurately work out your projected monthly income and expenses before your date of retirement (or soon after), and you subsequently discover that you likely will come up short on a regular basis, then the fear factor will undoubtedly kick in and may deliver a serious blow to your retirement happiness. In fact, it could easily transform your retirement happiness into fear, stress, and, ultimately, depression.[34]

Moreover, if you have not adequately planned your finances in a legally protected structure (seek legal advice, if necessary), then, if you unfortunately find yourself in some sort of diminished capacity, unable to look after your own finances, and you have to rely on someone else managing your checkbook, you will have the added concern of ensuring that your financial manager handles everything properly and honestly.

In other words, if your asset base is not secured by locked-in protection (e.g., company pension, if you have one), where your wishes are set in concrete for the rest of your life, then any deviation could be manipulated against you. Not nice but potentially realistic.

Case Study: *How important is it to understand what your income will be before you retire?*

Yvonne is a soon-to-be-retired dental hygienist. She has worked all her adult life and was married but got divorced about fifteen years ago. She says, "I am on my own, and I have some health issues, so to be honest, I don't know how long I might live, but my greatest fear right now is that if I live longer than what might be expected, will I have enough money to live comfortably? My health insurance will only go so far, and prescription [costs] will inevitably increase."

Yvonne is not alone in this predicament.

She will admit to herself that she came late to this retirement planning matter. She had relied on her then-husband to take care of those things, and when he left, she was slow in the uptake.

So much so that she says, "I'm so far behind in my pension strategy that I dread to look into it. I don't even

---

34. It is estimated that almost half of individual investors in the United States are concerned that they will outlive their savings in their retirement years and that Social Security will become their primary source of retirement income. Nanci Hellmich, "Big Retirement Fear: Outliving Your Savings," *USA TODAY*, accessed September 24, 2014, http://www.usatoday.com/story/money/personalfinance/2014/09/24/investors-fear-outliving-retirement-savings/16095591.

know if I have made all the contributions. So I went to see the pension people, and they were less than helpful, but they did tell me that if I made up a lump sum contribution, which is permitted in my country, then I would get so much monthly pension for the rest of my life, or I could take a lump sum payment back out at age sixty-five."

The problem would be if she lives way beyond her expected years, and the health problem is not as bad as expected. Then if she took the lump sum and invested it, her monthly income, given low interest rates, will not be enough to keep her going. On the other hand, if she opted for the monthly payments, then if she doesn't live as long as she would like, she is concerned that she will leave money on the table.

The essence of her plight is not only the pension dilemma but the broader issue—she simply did not look to the future when she was earning a good salary and didn't work out what savings she needed over the working years for her future retirement.

She admits that things like spreadsheets baffle her, and she would avoid even discussing her finances if she had a choice. Yet even a simple piece of paper and a pencil would have made the difference between retirement happiness and utter dejection.

Understanding Your Finances

Estimating your expenses is really not too difficult because you already know the basics—accommodation, groceries, insurances, utilities, and so forth. Finding out what pensions you will get is equally straightforward—you go ask.

All in all, the ability to add up one set of numbers and subtract them from another list of numbers would, in Yvonne's case, have shown her where she was headed. And more to the point, she would have found out years ago, in plenty of time to do something about it.

Before we address the psychological impact related to running out of money in retirement, we should recognize why, in many instances, people don't plan their financial future adequately or even at all. It may not just be due to laziness or that they can't be bothered.

Many retirees have inadequate financial literacy, which creates barriers to effective planning. The barriers can include the following:

- a fear of working with numbers, due to a lack of skill or experience
- having relied on a now-departed spouse for financial matters
- lack of knowledge and understanding of pension, investment, and banking products
- inability to fully comprehend inflation or compounding
- inability to fully appreciate the impact of longevity on financial resources
- being scared to face the shortfall reality too early

Overcoming Barriers

- Familiarize yourself with basic financial terminology.
- Meet with your pension provider, if you have one.
- Understand the differences between the various pension and retirement savings plans that are available in your country.
- Learn how to apply for your government pension payments well in advance of your retirement date.
- Find a financial advisor who can explain things to you in layman's terms.
- Join an online financial learning forum.
- Keep a spreadsheet of your financial position.
- Understand the tax regulations in your jurisdiction regarding your retirement income.

Most people look forward to retirement. We have been brought up to believe that our sunset years will be the best years of our lives and that we will be able to relax, play golf, travel, and spend more time with family.

But the harsh reality is that for many people, impending retirement, especially if mandatory, is a very worrying event in their lives. It's not just that money concerns may feature prominently in the future—after all, during their working lives, they probably ran into money problems many times—but that this time they have little if any potential to recoup shortfalls through employment income. They simply cannot foresee how they will fill the gap. This will typically create some level of anxiety—perhaps deep anxiety, perhaps leading to despair and perhaps depression.

BY FAILING
TO PREPARE,
YOU ARE
PREPARING TO FAIL
BENJAMIN FRANKLIN

You May Experience the Following

- a deflated feeling of needing to *take out* of your savings rather than *put in*, as you have done throughout your working years
- worries about not being able to pay for medications and/or hospital care, if insurances don't cover your costs
- concerns about not being able to adequately pay for housing, utilities, or groceries
- feelings of failure if you can't leave adequate inheritances for family
- being forced into selling your house and renting or downsizing
- having to seriously curtail your anticipated lifestyle
- not being able to maintain financial spending levels along with your friends
- throwing away or seriously downgrading your bucket list
- having no reserve fund for unexpected expenditures

For those of you not yet retired, the concern that you may not have enough money in retirement is most likely just an observation and certainly not yet an emotion. An observation is merely a recognition that something exists or *may* exist at some point in the future.

If we can emphasize the trauma associated with poor finances *in* retirement for those *approaching* retirement, we hopefully can persuade you to review your planning process; amend it, if need be; and closely monitor it as you get closer to your date of retirement.

Once you have crossed over the date of retirement, it may be too late to wake up and realize that your cash flow will not be adequate and that you will have to tap into your asset base, assuming you have one. It won't be possible to work overtime to save more or to get a second job to increase the retirement pot. It also is unlikely that, once in retirement, you will easily find part-time work. If you are fortunate to find something, the associated income likely will be way less than what you were earning in your preretirement job.

That sort of dilemma must be avoided at all costs, if possible. Looking forward to your retirement is one thing, but realizing that when you get there, you won't have enough money is quite something else. Prepare thyself.

Psychological Effects of Money Problems

- not being able to sleep properly or for any length of time
- not eating properly or only picking at food
- can't be bothered to get dressed in the morning
- feeling perpetually nauseated
- bringing on serious or chronic illness
- weight loss, headaches, lack of energy
- not being interested in family or grandchildren
- quarrels with your spouse
- not being interested in any social or community gatherings
- needing medical assistance and/or prescription medicines
- having no interest in self-help—exercise, diet, and well-being
- not wanting to depend on family or friends to come to your rescue
- not wanting to seek welfare assistance
- having feelings of despair or panic or being destitute

- feeling humiliated about seeking professional, medical, or financial help
- not enjoying the so-called good life in retirement

But of course, the greatest concern is if the negative factors turn into depression.

According to a report from the Institute of Economic Affairs (IEA), following an initial boost in health, *retirement increases your risk of clinical depression by 40 percent*, while raising your chances of being diagnosed with a physical condition by 60 percent. It also

- reduces your likelihood of being in self-reported excellent or very good health by 40 percent, and
- raises your risk of taking medication for a diagnosed physical condition by 60 percent.

Obviously, money concerns are not the only cause of depression, but financial distress is certainly a leading component and affects people regardless of their otherwise good health.

Too much credit card debt, too many loans, or having to still carry a mortgage "at this age" are potential contributors to a person's worries about money and that, if left unchecked or unresolved, can slide a person into depression. The burden of debt can cause sleepless nights and baggage that you might think would have been gone by now. The fact that debt is still hanging around can easily cause even the strongest, healthiest retiree to develop unwanted stress.

It is perhaps difficult for many of us to understand how a person not only can reach a level of frustration or worry due to money problems but of utter despair. It is probably even more difficult to comprehend how other factors get mixed into the despair equation—loneliness, poor health, feelings of hopelessness and that of time running out—and dramatically increase and compound the level of depression in a person's life.

Simple activities such as opening the mail, answering the phone, balancing your checkbook, paying your bills, keeping up-to-date with your credit cards, and so forth can be overwhelming for many people.

Depression is not a feature of getting older on its own. There will always be a catalyst. A state of depression can arise for several reasons, and obviously your health will be your first consideration and concern, but if your financial situation is in doubt, it will run a close second.

> "Money isn't all that's critical in life. My health and
> happiness are so much more important."

Hopefully, you will never have to test that statement.

Top Ten Tips for Your Journey

1. Financial planning for your retirement years is not up for discussion— it is life-critical.
2. Don't overspend in the early years of retirement. Take a balanced, long-term view.
3. Beyond pension and investment income, don't plan on any other income. If it happens, fine, but don't expect it.
4. Financial comfort underpins your retirement happiness.
5. Manage the money you have before the lack of it dictates and controls your lifestyle.
6. Watching your pennies is a fact of retirement life; embrace the idea.
7. Be careful of get-rich-quick schemes. You may not have time to recover.
8. Lend to family members wisely, if at all.
9. Rainy days are more prevalent in our latter years. Always have an umbrella handy.
10. Think young, act your age, and manage your money wisely.

CHAPTER 9

The Components of Your Preretirement Plan

Preretirement—Financial Planning

Depending on what age you are now, you may be properly set up in your company and state government pension plans and need only let the years to retirement roll forward until you are at the age to begin drawing a pension. On the other hand, you may not be well structured,[35] but you may still be young enough to make extra payments to catch up and get yourself back on track. If, however, you are nearing retirement or are already in retirement and are not well structured, then you have a lot of thinking to do about how you are going to fix this.

- The average person spends at least twenty years in retirement.[36] Biggest unknown is the denominator issue, or how long you will live—not how long you'd like to live or expect to live but just

---

35. A well-structured portfolio is one that is designed to stabilize your retirement funds so that your income generated from those funds will sustain your lifestyle for the duration of your life.

36. "Growing Older in America: The Health and Retirement Study," National Institute on Aging, National Institutes of Health, last modified January 22, 2015, https://www.nia.nih.gov/health/publication/growing-older-america-health-and-retirement-study/chapter-2-work-and-retirement.

how long you *will* live. In other words, if you divide your total retirement funds by the number of years that you expect to live, will the result provide adequate annual money to maintain your lifestyle?

- Fewer than half of Americans have calculated how much they need to save for retirement.[37]
- In 2012, 30 percent of private-industry workers with access to a defined contribution plan did not participate.

How did we get ourselves into this mess?

Part of the hesitation to plan for retirement is the word *retirement* itself. On the one hand, we all look forward to not going to work and so forth, yet we fail to accept that at that time we will be older. The word *retirement* conjures up feelings of being old, over the hill, past it, and so forth—we hesitate to use the word. We just don't want to think of ourselves as being old. Too bad. The clock is ticking whether we like to look at it or not.

"Retirement is something for my mum and dad."

The harsh reality of retirement life is (to use the old cliché) "If you fail to plan, you are planning to fail." There is no melodrama about this issue. If you have not adequately provided for your postwork finances, then you will, in all likelihood, have no way back, and you may be miserable for the remaining years of your life.

If you reckon that just because you have been contributing to your pensions throughout your working life they will easily take care of you in retirement, you may be in for a rude shock. Don't make assumptions until you get the facts, and even then, keep in mind that inflation, economic turbulence, unexpected expenses, or family emergencies and so forth could suddenly appear without warning. Obviously, it's hard to actually

---

37. "Saving for Retirement in America," 2006 RCS Fact Sheet, 2006 Retirement Confidence Survey, Employee Benefit Research Institute and Mathew Greenwald & Associates, Inc., accessed September 1, 2016, https://www.ebri.org/pdf/rcs06_fs_01_saving_final.pdf.

plan for *unexpected* events, but if you have the ability to build in some sort of cushion to your financial status, then do so. That extra contribution to your pension plan today could make a huge difference in years to come. Adjust your day-to-day spending now to accommodate more contributions.

Turning the Dream into Reality

The postwork world of our future selves is difficult for most of us to envisage, but … you really should make every effort to define a *desired* retirement lifestyle plan, and then work out what you will have to do now in order to ensure that you can afford it; then make any necessary adjustments.

This prediction exercise is complex and includes forecasting retirement income, forecasting retirement expenses, estimating current and future assets, estimating current and future liabilities, being conscious of unexpected expenses, estate planning considerations for your surviving spouse, leaving an inheritance, and any relevant tax implications for all the above. This plan should be reviewed regularly throughout your life and *especially during your Third Journey,* and not just as a list of things to do in the first year of retirement.

Most people can realistically only project forward for a maximum of five years. To plan longer than that is fine, but common sense dictates that the further out you look, the less certain you will be that you are correct. Any number of issues in your life will help you to properly plan in five-year retirement chunks.

- The kids will be married and will have left home by then (maybe!).
- The grandkids won't need you so much for pickups and so forth.
- Your energy levels will most likely change.
- Your attitude to your current everyday concerns will mellow as new issues emerge.
- Your peace of mind will slowly rise, and you will begin to view the future differently.

In other words, by reviewing reasonably known issues and how they will most likely play out, you can set your retirement lifestyle pattern for a period of time—but not indefinitely. You must remain cognizant that the aging process will change your circumstances and priorities, and it is wise to acknowledge this from the start.

If you have grandiose aspirations, and you can afford it, go for it. If you have grandiose aspirations but can't afford it, then you have a choice to make between going broke much sooner than you had planned or cutting back on your jet-set lifestyle. You must resist all temptations to blow the lot too soon.

Now that we have your attention, we will discuss some of the many aspects of the financial planning process, keeping in mind that they all fit together into one master plan and appreciate that by adjusting one aspect will inevitably affect many others.

Let's address the income side of your personal plan first.

In retirement, there will probably be two primary (and perhaps one secondary) sources of income. Pension income and investment income are the primaries, and part-time or full-time employment are the secondary.

As we discussed in the introduction, long before pension schemes were created, the working population just kept on working. They had no option. If they stopped working at a given age, and if they had not saved for that day, their livelihood became tenuous. A few people managed to put a little by for their old age, but most folks didn't. It wasn't a case of not caring about their futures but more because they barely had enough to live on while working—there just wasn't any to spare for savings.

Initially, the introduction of mandatory pension schemes by employers and state pension schemes by governments created mixed feelings in the general working population. On the one hand, they liked the idea of securing a retirement future financially, yet on the other hand, they didn't particularly like being forced to allocate part of their wages to make the required contributions. In other words, they had to face a today cost, rather than appreciate a tomorrow benefit.

Company Pensions

Broadly speaking, pension schemes nowadays are almost exclusively defined contribution (DC) schemes, where the employees pay most or all the contributions into their pension plans. Until a few years ago, the defined benefit (DB) scheme was the standard—where the employer paid most or all the contributions into the employee's pension plan, and on retirement the employee received a pension for life at realistic and sustainable levels, usually adjustable for inflation. Those days are largely gone worldwide.

Today, whatever you pay into your pension scheme is what you get back out, plus all accumulated investment income and increases in the fund's valuation over time. The contribution structure in the Western world is typically one where the *employee* pays about 5 percent of his salary into his pension scheme, and the *employer* will match that 5 percent into the same pot. The employer contribution will be fixed, but the employee will usually have the option to pay in more by way of voluntary contribution.

The purpose of this book is not to discuss the merits of various schemes available in different countries but rather to focus on the personal choices and the benefits of paying into whatever kind of scheme is available in your country.

The pension scheme will usually be investment-managed by a third-party professional investment management company (and not managed by the employer's staff). They will typically offer various levels of investment risk, ranging from conservative to higher risk, and typically within a mutual fund structure, where mutual funds are selected by the investment manager in a predetermined portfolio structure. The employee then chooses from the predetermined list of mutual funds. Choosing which investments to make and the overall percentage mix of the stocks in your portfolio is a complicated business, and it is unusual for employees to be granted full self-determination unless they happen to be investment professionals.

You must discuss all your options with your pension advisor and fully understand the differences between annuity and drawdown, not only in the immediate term after your retirement date but the long-term sustainability of your income stream and how it will affect your estate left for your family. This discussion is critical to your retirement finances and must be exhaustively investigated.

If the employee has the option to contribute to an employment-based pension scheme, then there is little doubt that the employee should join the scheme. It is a forced method of saving and will render acceptable financial benefits in later years. It may very well be the difference between a good retirement life and a poor one.

There is no time like ASAP to discuss the scheme in detail within your retirement planning exercise. It is essential to know all about the following:

- your current contribution levels, both mandatory and voluntary
- your current contributions and investment returns balance
- your type of investment choice, such as mutual funds
- your choices regarding type of pension (e.g., annuity or drawdown) on retirement
- your current approximate pension income at date of retirement

Government Pensions

If there is a government-controlled pension scheme in the country where you reside (e.g., the national pension scheme in the UK), you will probably have been automatically enrolled and required by law to contribute.

These schemes are very simple to follow in broad terms. There are contribution units to achieve to subsequently receive the full pension. If your contributions are less than the maximum level (due to not working for a period of time, for example), then your subsequent pension will be correspondingly less, on a proportionate basis. In some countries you may have the opportunity to make lump sum catch-up payments in subsequent years.

Usually, the amount of the pension is fixed by government and is probably inflation-indexed. In other words, once you have contributed the maximum amount, the pension benefit is the same for everyone.

Broadly speaking, government pension schemes were initially introduced to provide a safe and reliable source of income to the citizens of the country when they reached retirement. It was a forced-saving scheme in some respects. While the perennial complaint by pensioners is that they aren't receiving enough, the reality is that while the payments may not be wholly adequate to cover living expenses, they nonetheless are a welcome addition to the overall income levels of participants.

Investment Income

In this retirement planning phase, too many people almost disregard any investments they have built up over their working lives. In fact, too many people rely solely on their pension plans (see above) for their retirement projections. The justification is that living expenses are too tight as it is, and while contributions to pension plans are mandatory, further savings are not always possible. Fair point.

Keep in mind that even the smallest weekly or monthly deposit into a personal investment program will add up over time, and if the payments are treated as a cost of living rather than an extra savings payment, the investments may become not noticeable to your current living costs, and the accumulations may be very valuable by the time you reach retirement age.

It is almost redundant to say that the earlier you start your personal investing, the better you will be in your sunset years (assuming you don't have to withdraw from the program earlier due to some unexpected expense). Probably the best way to do that is to find, for example, a quality mutual fund investment company, pick one or more of their mutual funds, and start making regular contributions via automatic withdrawal from your salary—and then forget about it.

Obviously, in today's turbulent times and especially since the recent banking crisis, it is not wise to buy and then ignore the investment. An annual or semiannual review should always be part of your due diligence, year after year.

The choice of the type of mutual fund is really quite personal.

Do you prefer safe investments (e.g., government bonds, treasuries); or medium risk, such as corporate bonds; or higher risk, such as corporate equities?

Broadly speaking, the younger you are, the riskier you can be. That's not a rule, just a guideline. The theory is that if your investment goes down in value and doesn't look like it will recover in time to provide your retirement income as anticipated, then you have time to rebuild and restore its value. Obviously, the closer you are to retirement, the less time you have to refill the barrel.

The other advantage of the mutual fund investment type is that your fund will be managed by a professional investment manager (not you, or your uncle, or your best friend). But bear in mind that not every mutual fund manager gets it right all the time, and investments can go down as well as up. On the whole, however, the professional investment approach will work out.

Of course, you could be bold and manage your own investment portfolio, either in stocks or bonds or both.

If you feel comfortable enough to self-manage and if you have time to fix your mistakes, then go ahead. However, the guideline would be that if your self-investment management will heavily impact your retirement fund, then you must be much more careful and cautious. If, on the other hand, you like to play the markets, then, as long as you are not putting your family's financial future at risk, by all means enjoy yourself.

At the time of retirement, you have some options:

- You can stop contributing to your investment plan, and let the dividends/interest provide your retirement income.
- You can keep contributing into your investment plan, and increase your fund, thereby increasing your dividends/interest when you finally do need them.
- You can stop contributing into your investment plan and let value of the plan (hopefully) increase in value, and then cash out all or part of it in lump sums when you need it for retirement spending.

- You could begin to migrate your value-driven investments over to income-driven investments to provide you the cash flow. Staying in value-driven investments may allow you to increase your value, but until you cash out, your cash flow income will not start to flow. You may never need the assets, apart from major outlays for health, major repairs, and the like. Maintaining adequate cash flow income is really the primary goal in retirement. Having said this, don't convert *all* your assets. The conversion should only apply to enough value assets to produce the needed annual income. Save the rest of the value-based assets in your existing portfolio to continue to grow for a rainy day.

Home Equity

If you own your home and, in this retirement planning phase, still have a mortgage on the property, then as you approach retirement, you should make every effort to pay off your mortgage, if possible, as income will inevitably be much more limited and tight. In other words, paying the monthly mortgage payments while you are working and getting a regular income is fine, but when only your retirement income kicks in, it may not be as easy to direct your cash flows to a continuing mortgage.[38]

The property asset, typically the family home, is obviously one of your principal assets in your life and more so as you reach retirement. Your home will most likely be the largest part of your overall net worth, but in cash flow terms it is a *dormant asset*. Unlike investments in equities, mutual funds, bonds, or even pension plans, your home provides no cash flow benefits. Your asset is tied up, and you can't benefit from the increase in value from the time you bought it.

For example, let's say you bought your house several years ago for $100,000 (using a full mortgage of $100,000), and today it is worth $250,000. Meanwhile, your mortgage principal payments have reduced your mortgage liability by, say, $50,000 (thus, the remaining mortgage is now $50,000). Your net worth today is $200,000—your investment has doubled—*but …*

---

38. The word mortgage comes from the French *mortgage*; literally, death pledge. French peasants worked until they died for the privilege of owning a house.

If you need retirement income *cash flow,* this asset will not provide it for you. The net worth is correct but only on paper.

There are only two ways to liquidate some or all of your home equity; either sell and use the cash to *rent* a new place, or *downsize* to a dwelling that is cheaper than the value of your current home to free up *some* equity.

In the former, you swap your home equity for cash equity, so to speak, but bear in mind that because you are renting (paying money to a third party), your cash pot will be reducing. It may never be exhausted, depending on how long you live, but it will get less each rented year. Downsizing allows one property asset to be substituted by another property asset, thus maintaining your position in the property market. The excess cash (current property value less new property value) can be used for retirement income cash flows through a reinvested portfolio approach.

Those are the only options available to you, apart from some form of refinancing your mortgage or asset value (but that probably will incur continuing cash payments, so it may not be the best alternative) or renting out a portion of your dwelling to a tenant, if your home is configured in such a way that this is possible.

One other option that has become more popular over the last few years is the *reverse mortgage,* which allows you to convert part of the equity in your home into cash without having to sell your home. But keep in mind that a reverse mortgage will use up the equity in your home, which means fewer assets for you and your heirs. The traditional home mortgage means that you pay the lender, such as a bank, your mortgage payment every month to buy your home over the duration of the mortgage (typically twenty years). In a reverse mortgage, the lender pays *you* the loan. Reverse mortgages take part of the equity in your home—a kind of advance payment on your home equity over the remaining course of your life from the date you take out the reverse mortgage.

The reverse mortgage is ideal if you have substantial equity built up in your property, and allows you to release some of that equity over time to provide you with cash flow income, year after year. You never lose title to the property, and on your passing or when the property is otherwise sold, the reverse mortgage is closed out. Depending on where you live, there will be terms and conditions that apply, such as a minimum age (typically, sixty-two) when you can negotiate and commence a reverse mortgage.

It is strongly advised that you consult a qualified financial advisor or bank manager before you do this, and do not solely seek the advice of a seller of reverse mortgages.

The only other means of liquidating occurs when you pass away and thus have no further need for the home, leaving it to your family to sell the property and take the cash (assuming they don't also live in the house or would do so when you pass). Keep in mind also that if inheritance is important to you, and if you can otherwise sustain your retirement lifestyle cashwise, then holding on to the higher-valued property means a higher inheritance value when you pass. Inheritance taxes may apply in your country as well, so bear that in mind also.

Working in Retirement

Easier said than done, probably.

The employment market these days tends to imagine that your education, intelligence, and experience disappear overnight when you retire. You go to bed smart and wise, and wake up stupid, in the eyes of others.

If you intend to seek new employment (other than with your current preretirement employer), your chances of working with your existing skill sets are fairly slim (unless you happen to be trained in a field where you can operate your own small business as a sole proprietor and take on the volume of customers required to make ends meet.) It can be a harsh reality, but it is typically correct. Jobs are scarce in the work world, and they don't want you competing for them anymore.

If, however, you choose to downsize your aspirations, and go to work in the local grocery store, Walmart, or gas station, where your skill sets are largely not required, then your chances improve somewhat. Dropping down from a high income rate to a very low income rate doesn't appeal to everyone, but the nonmonetary pleasures of continued working and meeting people can easily be the justification to accept the lower income.

Moreover, if your retirement spending is covered by all your pension and investment income, and you can live comfortably on that, then this extra income can be welcome play money. Just make sure that this additional income does not adversely affect your income tax position by bumping you into a higher tax bracket than you budgeted for.

In the preretirement planning stage, the time frame for getting postretirement employment is probably obscured. Unless you have agreed with your current employer that you will continue for some amount of time after you officially retire, the opportunities for new employment will only appear once you enter the postwork world.

Obviously, there are issues regarding postretirement employment other than just money. Do you really just want to relax and unwind, or do you feel you still have some good years left in you, and the thought of quitting cold turkey doesn't appeal? Maybe a slower slide to full time retirement would work best for you.

There are physical and psychological issues to consider as well. If you are in your midforties, say, then your energy and motivations will be quite strong. No thoughts of stopping. But you have to think forward and imagine what you might feel like twenty years from now. Because that is almost impossible to foresee, most people ignore the issue completely and simply don't think about their ability or willingness to work once they have crossed the retirement threshold. Fair enough. But you should always keep in the back of your mind that when you actually retire, you may not be interested in more work. Therefore, if your financial forecasting includes some form of part-time income, you must be certain that your arithmetic is not heavily dependent on extra income. You may not be able or willing to fulfill that income source indefinitely.

Now let's turn to ...

Expenses

Daily living

Everyone's lifestyle is different. While some people may want to travel extensively in retirement, others may choose to stay at home and garden. Also, we may not all feel that we want to travel economy class now that we've reached the golden years—a little bit of luxury may be the new standard.

But regardless of which level of spending you want to run with in retirement, the constituent parts of everyone's daily life are broadly the same—we all need a roof over our heads, food to eat, heat to warm us, water, electricity, clothing, transportation, and medical insurance. The costs of these can vary significantly between one retiree and another. One retiree may want a big roof, some may want a downsized roof, while some may even want two roofs—one here and one there (a vacation home to flee to when winter starts to approach, for example).

Thus, your preparation of an expense budget is very personal. The only safe guideline would be to make sure you have covered all known and expected expenses and have adequately projected their cost. Don't try to artificially squeeze the costs downward simply to provide more fictitious headroom versus your income. That is false accounting, which will come back and haunt you in later life. Be realistic in everything. If you don't know what something will cost in years to come, then take a swing at it, research online, or ask someone. But get as good a figure as you can.

If you can find a plausible guideline to assess the impact of inflation over the next ten or twenty years, go ahead and factor it in. But as long as you err on the side of too much in your budgeting, then the impact of inflation may not be too severe.

One last point on inflation: when inflation statistics are released by the government, the basket of goods and services used in their calculations will probably differ from your personal basket. For example, if you still have a mortgage and if it is a fixed mortgage (i.e., same payment of principal and interest each month through closure), then there is no inflationary impact on your accommodation costs. So maybe the official rate of inflation is on the high side in your situation. In any event, if you do use a rate, use the official one, just to be on the safe side.

Lastly, there may be certain expenses that change on retirement. Items such as public transport and other community services may have discounts for retirees. If they do, use them. You deserve them (and you paid for them, after all).

Although some costs usually decrease as you age, due to a natural tendency to live a simpler, more sedentary life, a few costs likely will increase—most importantly, the cost of health insurance. If you qualify for subsidized government coverage, then make sure the benefits are what you need—on retirement and especially in the longer-term future. You may not be healthy all of your retirement life. You may also have the option to stay in your employer's health plan, even though you are no longer working there, and enjoy the same benefits—albeit you may have to pick up a higher percentage of the premiums than you had while in employment. The fact that you *have* coverage (either through your employment situation or the government) is wonderful, but you simply *must* double- and triple-check that your coverage does not diminish as you get older, or if it does diminish, then be fully aware of what that means on retirement and for every year thereafter. You must also be fully aware of any extra costs you must pay as you age, extra premiums to be assessed if you have an illness, or increased deductibles. Health insurance is a critical, life-impacting issue, and it must be fully understood and accounted for. There are no half measures.

Other insurances must be considered as well—car, house, contents, travel, and so forth.

The issue of life insurance in retirement can be a quandary. On the one hand, when you expire, you don't get any benefit, but your spouse and/or family will benefit. Of course, that may be reason enough to have life insurance and to continue to pay life insurance premiums up to and beyond retirement. Most people keep paying the premiums and probably rightly so. But once you are in retirement, you may wish to review that.

In other words, if the payout on death is on the low side (i.e., not enough sum insured), and if the premiums keep rising due to your increasing age, then the cost-benefit analysis may not be as attractive in retirement as it seemed when you were younger. Having life insurance when you are in your midyears, especially when you have a young family, is a great idea. But as you get older, and the family moves out from the home and stands on its own feet, and your standard of living is fine, and the remaining spouse will *otherwise* be financially secure, then the cost of the insurance, in cash flow terms, may make the continuation to pay *less* attractive. If the lump sum settlement on your death won't make much of a difference to your overall net worth (your estate), but the cost of the insurance is a drain on your cost of living cash flows during the retirement years, then you may want to reconsider retaining your life insurance. It can be an emotive issue. When you discuss it with your insurance agent, he certainly will tell you you'd be a fool to stop it (of course), but you should weigh the financial considerations with the lifestyle and psychological issues. It is really very personal but worth a review and reevaluation.

Expected or unexpected expenses

Many large-ticket items can be encountered in retirement. Once the income and assets have been determined and their sustainability assured, then sometimes the retirement years are an ideal time to "splash the cash" and fulfill one of your lifelong dreams:

- adding more rooms to the house (the grandkids are coming for the weekend!)
- doing some long-awaited repairs to the house
- buying a second home for vacation purposes
- buying that RV, boat, motorcycle, or riding lawn mower
- buying that flashy new SUV and fitting it with every tech gimmick imaginable
- going on that around-the-world trip (maybe not every year but once, for sure)
- buying a bed-and-breakfast place or a little shop (or a big shop)
- building that train set to run through the entire house (much to the consternation of your spouse and the family dog)
- buying a new pair of shoes doesn't count, but buying a walk-in closet to house your shoe collection does

Despite all the available information, most of us do operate on the idea that life will proceed without interruption in retirement if we have done our planning correctly. Granted, some events cannot be anticipated, and a sudden change in health is often one of them. If some chronic illness or accident occurs, and you are not otherwise fully covered by health insurance, then your pocket will take the hit. The severity of the hit can easily mean the difference between an expected comfortable retirement and a horrible one, where the time left to live becomes an enormous burden. ("If I live another ten years, how will I ever be able to cover my daily costs or any further large expense?")

Not a pleasant place to find yourself in at this stage of life.

But many other potential unexpected costs can arise. Serious property damage, if uninsured. Family emergencies through loss of the main provider in the household, yet with kids to feed and bring up.

How do you forecast these unexpected costs, much less pay for them? These are simply unpredictable, not only in their occurrence but in their timing and cost.

There is no easy answer.

Case Study: *Will long-term disability sustain me if I have to retire early due to injury?*

Paul lives in Vancouver and worked as a painter all his adult life. He worked for a medium-sized company in the local area and was smart enough to contribute into their pension plan from the day he started. In fact, he took the option of extra contributions.

"All was fine," he says, "until about six years ago when I slipped off a ladder onto a concrete area. It was a cold, wet day, with lots of leaves around. I thought I had placed the bottom of the ladder correctly, but when I had gone up only three or four rungs, the whole thing slid from underneath me, and I injured my lower back.

"I worked for another few months, but the pain was very bad, and frankly, I couldn't do the job to my satisfaction, so I was forced into taking early retirement. I had been one of those people who loved to work with spreadsheets and financial projections, so I thought my retirement planning was well in hand. I had always assumed that I would work and make pension contributions for another ten years."

"Meaning that the pension contributions stopped?"

"Yes, they had to. I wasn't working. I did get some

disability pension, but that's not very much, and I had to start taking the normal pension out every month for living expenses. So I was hit financially three times. First, I lost my employment income. Second, the pension contributions from my employer and me stopped. Third, instead of the pension fund accumulating investment value, I had to start withdrawing from the fund," he said. "I manage to make ends meet, but things are really tough, and I have years and years ahead of me."

A work related injury can permanently alter your entire retirement. In Paul's case, the long-lasting financial implications proved to be more serious than his physical injury. This proves that you can never save too much for your retirement.

Your health is your most valuable asset. Take good care of it.

Discretionary Spending

If you have assets that are superfluous to your income-generating needs— half of your assets, for example, generate the required income to live comfortably, and the other half provide value opportunities or simply excess income—then you should have sufficient assets, all things being equal, to cover most unexpected situations. You wouldn't face severe life-changing financial problems in that scenario, although your cushion would be reduced. This is something you should definitely keep in mind when considering making dream expenditures.

Clearly, if this big expenditure is beyond your immediate means or, more to the point, if it is affordable today but will impact your income generation by selling assets to cover the cost in years to come, then you have to give serious consideration to whether you can afford it, or whether you should revise your idea and structure it one piece at a time, or just do a simplified version of it altogether. The notion that you are in retirement and you deserve it is a nice idea, but it may not be practical. And what do you do if you live much longer than you thought?

These expenses are all by-choice expenses. You have (hopefully) worked out that you can afford it and that your future income will not be diminished. If you can afford them, then by all means go ahead and enjoy yourself a bit (you *do* deserve it!).

We hope this section has armed you with a list of things to consider and research further as you clarify your retirement lifestyle plan. Keep in mind that the Internet is a great source of information (both good and bad), and it is important to find a financial advisor to guide your decision-making process. Equally so, it is important to maintain an emergency fund and not lose sight of the fact that unexpected events can and do happen in the Third Journey. Never ignore the importance of making sure that your income and expenses are in sync with each other.

Preparing a Budget

Having covered both income and expenses separately, it's now time to bring them together and develop the forecast for your retirement life—the budget.

It's reasonable to say that preparing a budget, especially if you want to do it in computer spreadsheet format, doesn't come naturally to many people and can seem a daunting task at first.

It might be tempting to skip this step, but you really must make every effort to determine your income and your expenses when you will be in your golden years and record them regularly. It is too melodramatic to say that it is a matter of life or death, but you are definitely playing Russian roulette with your future if you have no idea whether you are financially prepared or not—especially when you are still working and probably have the time to fix things by making up any projected shortfall. You won't get much chance to fill the gap once you are retired. *You can't put the toothpaste back in the tube!*

So let's get started.

First, a budget is a projection only, not a hard-and-fast plan to be followed to the letter. It is a guideline at best—a very, very important one in this case of retirement planning, but it can and inevitably will move up and down as financial facts unfold. But you simply must know *before* you enter retirement if you will be able to sustain the retirement lifestyle you choose, given your projected income and expenses.

Now, open a new Excel document or at least draw a column on a clean piece of paper (if you like to do things old school), and make a list of all your anticipated expenses, starting with your daily living costs—accommodation, utilities, groceries, transportation, clothing, credit cards, and so forth—for an entire year. You can do this any way you like, but it is probably easiest to work on a monthly basis, and if you have any quarterly or annual expenses (such as home or auto insurance), then divide it into monthly pieces. Keep in mind, though, that in terms of cash flow, such costs are actually paid quarterly or monthly, so your monthly cash flows will be higher in certain months and lower in other months of the year. (Don't forget to add the cost of Christmas and annual family vacations, if you traditionally participate in these events.)

Simply add up the monthly expenses to get the total and then add in a factor for the unexpected. As that amount is completely unknown, it is impossible to predict with any accuracy, but for the time being, simply enter it as a line item to be filled in shortly after we have covered your income.

Insert all your *income* sources and amounts—again, if some come in quarterly or annually, for the purposes of this budgeting exercise, divide the amounts into monthly parts. If you have investment income in cash, such as dividends or interest, which don't add increases in value, then use a best-guess estimate, as your time frame may be too far out to be completely accurate.

If you can be certain that you will either keep on working in one way or another and thus will definitely receive postretirement employment income, then add it in. If you are not sure if you will get employment but are hopeful, then don't add it in. This is far too important to rely on hope.

Keeping the Boat Afloat

Now that you have all your income and expenses listed, the difference is the *surplus* or *deficit* each month.

This will tell you if you will be solvent in your postwork life as you currently envisage it, or whether your income will fall short of your dreams. Also bear in mind that even if it looks like you will have enough income to keep yourself afloat, you need to think about putting something in reserve for unexpected expenses. As said above, there is no accurate method to do that, so the best you can determine, if you are in surplus, is that you have enough surplus to withstand a big hit.

Part of that determination is whether you save the surplus each month in a separate savings account, which will build up over time, or whether you extra-spend and use it up. If you spend it, then your reserve will be small. Moreover, you don't know when the big hit will occur, and you could get caught short.

If the big hit is a planned expense, then you can simply save the surplus for several months and then take the hit. If it is unexpected (not planned), then negotiate the best payment terms that you can, and try to pay it off in installments using your monthly surplus. Avoid paying out capital savings, if at all possible.

On the other hand, if your budget shows a monthly *deficit*, you have some serious thinking to do. The sooner you prepare your budget to find out if you are projecting a deficit, the more time you will have to rearrange your finances to get things fixed before you leave the work world. That may be easier said than done, of course, but at the very least, you now know what lies ahead in retirement. If you predict a deficit, then the fact that it will probably be in deficit for the rest of your life (and will also accumulate over time) means that you either have to cut back on your expected retirement lifestyle or find new income sources now or in retirement (e.g., keep on working, downsize, and so on). Don't rely on taking out bank loans—they are hard to obtain and even harder to service if you don't have a full-time job. The bottom line is simple: you won't be able to sustain yourself if you are predicting a deficit.

The last point to make with regard to a projected deficit is that sometimes you hear the old phrase, "You have to speculate to accumulate"—in other words, you might consider that today, while you are still working and earning, an investment in a new business for your retirement makes sense.

It might, but it depends a great deal on the particular investment that you are considering.

Be extremely careful not to take a high-risk investment that may drain your "today retirement pot" or require continual future capital investments that will be hard to achieve, further reduce your income in retirement, and worsen your deficit. Be very careful.

Final Words on the Budget

Don't ignore doing projections completely or leave it until later. The sooner you have an idea of where you will be financially, the better you will be in retirement. The notion that it will work out somehow is not a plan—it is only a hope, if not just a dream.

If you've never prepared a budget, you may shy away from using the word, or you may just not fancy doing one, but you must rethink and get down to it. Your lifestyle, your health and happiness, your family life, and more all critically depend on knowing if you can afford your retirement.

As Nike would say, "Just do it."

Top Ten Tips for Your Journey

1. Recognize that retirement income is, generally speaking, fixed income.
2. Be very clear about your pension income, not just at the start of your retirement but throughout.
3. If you are unsure of the sustainability of your investment income, seek professional advice.
4. Prepare a clearly defined budget well in advance of your retirement. The word budget tends to put people off. Don't be put off; it's important.
5. Pay off as many liabilities (e.g., mortgage) as you can while you are still earning a regular income.
6. In the five to ten years before retirement, push as much extra money as you can into savings. If your forecasts show that you will be in deficit each month, stop and review everything and make adjustments.
7. Understand that the phrase *cost of living* literally means how much you need to spend to enjoy your retirement lifestyle.

8. Realize that once you are retired, you can't go back and work extra hours to get more money.

9. Always compare your actual spending at the end of the year to your budget from the beginning of that year.

10. Think young, act your age ... and save hard.

CHAPTER 10

Managing Your Finances in Retirement

Postretirement—Adjusting and Managing Your Finances

Elsewhere in this book we have addressed the changes in lifestyle that you will experience after your date of retirement, including the psychological impacts. In this section, we will focus on the financial changes you might experience and how such changes may affect your comfort level and happiness.

Once you are in retirement, the game changes.

Not only are the rules different, but how you think about your financial future can be quite an eye-opener. The budgeting exercise that we went through in the previous chapter was based on projected income and expenses. At best, they were forecasts only. Once you cross through the retirement threshold, it is critical that you immediately compare these projections with the income that you actually receive.

You soon will realize that you no longer have a weekly paycheck or easy opportunities to increase your income and that you actually have to live on your pension, which is often only half to three-quarters of what you previously earned. It is always wise to acknowledge that the best of budgeting will be close but not exactly accurate, so no need to panic. The projections will be different from the realities but hopefully not too different. Inevitably, there will be expenses you completely forgot about and expenses that are higher (or lower) than projected. There also will be areas of your life where you decide to spend more than you had previously thought you would want to spend, such as a vacation home or a larger car.

Frugal Is the New You

Your entire attitude about money, especially about spending it, changes. You may not become a miser overnight, but you inevitably will be much more conscious of the cost of living than perhaps you were when working. Combining cash-management concerns with the realization that you are older now and that these are your latter years can create a rather unsettling feeling, which you probably never experienced before.

The words you will find you use more in retirement than in the previous years are "What?" and "How much?"

One of the nice things, though, about using those words is that because you might look like a retiree (the gray-hair syndrome), young folks smile and act like it's completely normal for you to ask for the senior discount or the early bird special, so you don't need to worry that anyone will think you are a cheapskate.

In fact, you'll probably find that you use these words in nearly every conversation with a salesperson, from buying the daily newspaper to buying an airline ticket. You will rapidly get into the habit of asking for the senior discount. So much so that if a hotel chain doesn't offer senior discounts, you'll quickly look for one that does. It's natural and totally acceptable to do that. Never be afraid to ask, and never be afraid to challenge vendors—if they want your business, they will listen and maybe change their minds.

Obviously, there are many established senior discounts—local area transit, for example. While it is a nice idea to avail yourself of the discounts, the chances are that if you haven't been used to traveling by bus or train, even though it is now much cheaper, it may not suit your lifestyle. Don't be vexed about not taking the benefit. You can only do what suits you and makes you happy.

Case Study: *Does it matter whether you stick to your monthly budget in retirement?*

Robert is one of those fastidious people who analyze every aspect of his life but sometimes has trouble making decisions and is prone to procrastinating on financial planning issues because he is fearful of making the wrong decision. He retired about three years ago from a fairly well-paid job in the office supplies business but is in financial difficulty already.

"I'm running out of cash. I have been overspending big time, and now I realize that I will have to stop eating for three months with no electricity, just to stop the rot and catch up." He's joking, of course, but the point is that in retirement the cash flow matter is the all-important one. As they say, "Cash is king." Never more true than in retirement.

His pension funds are safe, in that he hasn't dipped into the principal. Likewise, he has thus far not needed to dip into his investment portfolio. But the cash that flows from those sources—pension income and dividends or interest income—are not sufficient to keep him afloat month by month at his current rate of spending.

"The simple fact is that when I was working, there were months when I was in a shortfall, but I knew that in a week or so or at the end of the month, I would be getting more than enough to cover the shortfall and live normally. I may have had to scrimp a little bit on luxuries for a month or so, but the basics were covered. And if I needed to ask for a bank overdraft, my salary was enough proof that I could pay it back on time. Now, the problem is that I am on a fixed income, and there is no way to get tide-me-over monies."

In retirement, we all want to enjoy ourselves and do things we've always wanted to do, but procrastinating is not an accomplishment. If we throw caution to the wind and buy too many things or go on very expensive vacations, without first checking the cash flows over the next several months, for example, we may easily find ourselves in shortfall, if not free fall, with not much opportunity to have a safety net.

It may be easy to find some part-time work to bolster the cash flows, but in retirement the chances of getting something are fairly slim. It's fine to rely on the expectation that part-time work will come along and, as such, to figure it into the cash flow projections before retirement—unless that part-time supplement never materializes.

A shortfall in retirement, particularly if it is month after month, is a serious issue.

All Expenses Considered

Every single aspect of your life relating to money will become a consideration. A mini-calculation will jump into your conscious mind every time you spend money. Even simple things—like, "Do I really need another coffee?"—will come into play. There's no melodrama on this issue; it is real. For some retirees, it may be less of a consideration than for others, but don't be surprised when you start to question your own spending habits. We all do it. We really do.

The balance between "I'm in retirement, and I deserve to treat myself" and "I won't spend that amount of money on that" will become second nature to you. The dilemma will arise all the time. Another word that you will find yourself using a lot is *frugal*. This was a word you may have rarely used while working, maybe even didn't know what it meant, and certainly didn't consider it when you had regular, stable income.

"We're not cheap; we're frugal," you will start to say.

In some respects, retirement living can be less expensive than during your working life. Your commute travel costs will have been slashed, your gas bill for the car should be less, your lunch tab will be less, perhaps your wardrobe costs will be less, and there won't be after-work drinks and so forth. On the other hand, you may see an increase in some utility bills, such as electricity, if you are spending more time at home. But generally, the cost of living for the basics will be less. Your grocery bill may not change that much, unless your frugal new lifestyle starts to control your eating habits. The economy pack will seem more attractive than the supersized.

The frugal issue likely will cause some friction between you and your spouse. It is fair to say that the husband will look for the cheaper cuts while the wife knows that cheap doesn't work out well every time. By having much more time to cruise the grocery store, the price-comparison exercise becomes a hobby. Very few people in retirement will throw everything into the shopping cart without looking at the price. The rest of us will compare price to size or volume. We will start to discover that buying in bulk works out cheaper on a per-unit basis, but having a year's supply of Rice Krispies is perhaps not the best way to save money after all.

Should You Downsize?

If you are facing a budget shortfall then the idea of downsizing may come into play. This is an emotional and a financial matter, and there are a variety of things to consider. You've lived in this house for the past thirty years, you like it, it's convenient for everything you do, and you have adjusted your lifestyle to its best advantage for your needs. So why move?

There are two primary reasons why people consider moving. One is *financial*, and the other is *physical*. If you did your projections correctly in the planning phase, then your cost of housing will have been factored in, and all things being equal, you will be comfortable that your costs are manageable. Nonetheless, you may feel that you could make better use of your home equity by downsizing and releasing some of the equity into more liquid investments for more cash flow. Obviously, if you don't need the extra cash flow, then there is no desperate need to think about downsizing, apart from its being a nice idea to have some extra cash for the luxuries of life.

But when combined with the *physical* aspects of downsizing—the existing house may be too much to upkeep, with repairs, maintenance, cleaning, painting, and so forth—it could be a win/win situation. Downsize to a smaller, easier-to-manage property and release some equity. Then invest the released cash, less the cost of the new place, and receive greater cash flow income.

If it were that easy to downsize, we'd all give it serious consideration, but it isn't.

Can you actually sell the existing place? Will you get the price you need? Will the new place be cost-effective? Over and above the financial and physical issues, there are psychological issues to take into serious consideration.

Moving house can be a traumatic event for most people. It becomes even more traumatic as we age. We have emotional ties to the existing property, and the clever idea to downsize can turn really sour very quickly—and by then, it's too late to go back to the old place. The impact of moving becomes a very serious matter if you find out that you are not completely comfortable psychologically *after* you've moved. Stress, anxiety, and even depression are all results that we should avoid, but if we jump into the move simply for the financial and physical benefits, without giving deep thought to the mental side of the move, we could be in serious trouble.

Two obvious options to downsizing are moving in with family or to a retirement community, but can you manage to live in harmony with your children, even if they have invited you to live with them? Or can you tolerate the nosey social circles of most retirement communities, even if the assisted living services they offer are attractive? The choices can be both daunting and complicated.

Downsizing of any sort is not something to be rushed into. Consider your needs and options carefully so that when the right property becomes available, you can make a move, confident in the knowledge that you will be happy in your new place once you get settled.

What's on Your Bucket List?

In the planning phase, the idea that when you are in retirement—let's say ten years from *now*—you will travel and travel and travel can sometimes change direction when you're older (those ten years will take their toll). The wild adventurer in you may cause you to rethink the itinerary.

Clearly, your Third Journey *is* the time to enjoy the traveling to new places, so it is *not* inevitable that your older years will cause you to slow down—in fact, quite the opposite. This is the time to realize those dreams and get on the road. Don't sit back and let the world drift by without you.

Perhaps some of your plans *have* changed now that you are retired, and your desire to climb the Himalayas isn't quite the top priority anymore. That's perfectly fine. Aging does have a habit of changing minds. But also, now that the financial realities are staring you in the face, it is quite possible that your real time budgeting is making you reconsider some of those travel plans. Again, perfectly reasonable.

It is not uncommon to scale back some of the exotic plans you had in the planning phase. Maybe you should go for two weeks, not a month. Maybe you should fly economy, not first class. Maybe you should rent a smaller car, not a huge SUV. Maybe you should choose economical meal plans, not *haute cuisine*. The choices are yours and yours alone.

Simply be aware that being in retirement is very different from thinking about it.

It is not a climb down if you decide to be more frugal and cost-conscious now that you are seeing the real cash flows and are much clearer about the denominator effect than you were years ago. In fact, it is wise and very prudent to rethink your travel plans—but if you decide to stay with them as planned and can afford them, then you are in great shape, and you must do it. Simple as that.

Supplementing Your Income

You may feel that part-time employment should be part of your retirement life. Many emotional and family issues are associated with some form of extended employment after your retirement, but for the moment, let's focus on the financial aspects.

Within your budget exercise in the retirement planning phase, if you realized that you *must* have part-time income, then you have no wiggle room now that you are in retirement. In other words, based on your projections, if you simply *must* get part-time work, then you are placing heavy pressure on yourself to deliver. Of course, if you agreed with your preretirement employer that you would continue working with them, then you should be able to secure the income. Perhaps you found work with another employer before retirement, such that your projections were realistic at the planning phase.

If, however, you merely projected part-time work and factored it into your budget but didn't actually establish where the income would come from, then your budgeting may need to be reviewed. Now that you are retired and looking for work, it may not be as easy as you thought. Hopefully not, but reality can sometimes surprise all of us.

It would be even worse if your projected income and expenses had been based on part-time income, and that without such income your budgeting showed a shortfall, leading to a monthly deficit. Changes should have been made at that planning stage, because accounting for part-time income based on the *belief* you will get part-time work is a gamble.

Therefore, if now, in retirement, you can't find part-time work, but your budget must have it to balance, what do you do?

There is no easy answer.

You will have to scale back your expenses if your budget is tight. You cannot run at a monthly loss, certainly not for any length of time. But if your budget is able to withstand a no-part-time-income situation due to ample cushion, then it simply means that your surplus will be less than projected. You may decide to do some scaling back, just to preserve some cushion, but overall your lifestyle should not be greatly impacted. By and large, you should still be able to do most things as planned—maybe just not to the same degree or intensity.

Lastly, if you do get part-time employment, and factor it into your budget now that you are retired, then recognize that it may not be sustainable for a variety of reasons, and if you project too far out, then your cash management may be adversely affected down the line. Don't assume too much or too far ahead.

Keeping on Track

Monitoring your budget can be a fun exercise, but it can also be a nuisance at times. When the income and expenses are running as planned, your feelings of financial security will be high. However, if certain expenses change significantly—due to miscalculation, for example, or increases from the vendor—then your happiness level can drop.

It is important to monitor the budget cash flows against actual cash flows on a regular, scheduled basis. It is equally important, though, to not get paranoid or obsessive about your budget checking. You are in retirement and would like to be happy, but you find that the numbers aren't working out as planned, then the impact on your overall well-being can be significant.

Some people will ignore the monitoring completely and live on the basis that things will work out—and it is possible that indeed things will work out, but the wise retiree will pay attention to the numbers to ensure that surprises don't pop up. In any given month, if one expense is higher than expected, it can sometimes be fun to figure out which other expense can be lowered for that month to provide overall balance. The trick is to not be so deep into the budgeting process that your life is controlled by the numbers. If you go over one month, then so be it. If you go over every month, you need to reconfigure.

The following chart illustrates how concerned the average retiree is with a variety of everyday expenses and financial issues:

Americans' Top Financial Concerns—Gallup Poll 2014 Question: How concerned are you about each of the following matters, based on your current financial situation?		
	Very worried/ Moderately worried	Not too worried/ Not at all worried
	%	%
Not having enough money for retirement	59	35
Not being able to pay medical costs in the event of a serious illness	53	45
Not being able to maintain the standard of living you enjoy	48	52
Not having enough money to pay off your debt	40	48

Not being able to pay medical costs for normal health care	39	57
Not having enough to pay your normal monthly bills	36	62
Not having enough to pay for your children's college	35	31
Not being able to pay your rent, mortgage, or other housing costs	31	64
Not being able to make minimum credit card payments	16	65

Managing a Surplus

If you have organized your pension sources properly before retirement, then you should simply wait for them to roll in.

If your monthly income is actually in excess of your living needs, then if you have the option to scale back your pension payments, you might consider doing that, thereby leaving your retirement pot in professional investment hands and still growing through investment increases. If there is no such option, then take the full pension amount, use only what you need, and deposit the excess into a separate savings account. You never know when you might use it for extra luxuries or build up the reserve for unexpected expenses.

If you have surplus income from multiple sources it might be best to consult an experienced investment advisor regarding strategic reinvestment of that surplus and how to take advantage of any tax-saving vehicles that are available in your country.

Tightening Your Belt

So what happens if you find that your budgeting was way off, and now, in retirement, you realize that you are not able to pay for your expenses, assuming that you don't have part-time income, don't have much chance of getting part-time work, and your current income is fixed?

Realistically, you can only rethink the expense side of your budget. "Tighten the belt." "Scale back."

If your shortfall is considerable, you will need to seek any sort of job to get more money—menial tasks included. You simply can't sustain month over month shortfalls.

However, if your shortfall is fairly manageable or is temporary, you can make lots of compromises to get yourself back on track and stay there:

- Cut back on your grocery bills. Reset the monthly allocation and stick to it. You will easily adapt to less food without starving.
- Be mindful of utility usage. Turn off the lights when not in the room. It will mount up if you do that all the time.
- Don't make unnecessary journeys. Get relatives and friends to come to see you.
- If you had planned to take two trips this year, have a staycation instead, and treat yourself to some delicious takeout or a massage.
- If you had planned to be away for a month, go away for a week.
- If you normally go to the high-end salon every week, try the no-frills haircutting shop.
- If you normally get plants from the garden center, try growing them yourself from seeds.
- Look for senior discounts everywhere, and use them.
- If you eat out a lot, try going out for breakfast or for dessert and coffee, instead of a three-course meal.

Refinancing

But what do you do if, after all the above, you are still coming up short?

First, be clear whether the shortfall is short-term or permanent. If it's short-term, then perhaps try for a bank loan or family loan to see you over the tough period. You would need to add the loan repayments, including interest, into your budget going forward.

But if it is more severe and perhaps more permanent, then you will have to find alternative ways to refinance yourself.

There are two main refinancing options open to you (in your personal circumstances, there may be more):

- Refinance your mortgage or downsize, as discussed.
- Take capital out of your asset fund (e.g., sell some shares and take the cash as your self-lending).

These are serious changes to your game plan, so they must be researched and analyzed in great detail. You should *only* consider doing these after thorough checking of your cash flow position. You will have great difficulty in replacing the funds going forward. These will impact your expenses by excess mortgage payments not previously accounted for and also by lowering your cash flows from investments. The release of principal must be tightly controlled so as to avoid spending it on other costs ... or worse, thinking that now that you have excess cash you can go back to the splash-the-cash approach.

The broad rule of thumb for taking out principal from your investments is that you can comfortably take 3–4 percent of your total principal value each year. The rule merely provides a guideline in the event that you *do* need to augment your income flows from principal amounts. It suggests that you should not exceed 3–4 percent of the principal, which would equate to twenty to thirty years of retirement life before you completely run out of principal (leaving aside inflation, reinvesting of dividends, interest, or recurring value changes—up or down).

Also keep in mind to consider the denominator effect in the refinancing solution. If you expect to run at a shortfall for a few years, but your refinancing provides relief for, say, only half of that period (which you don't know at the time of the refinancing), but you live longer and still otherwise run a deficit, then you may be forced into a second round of refinancing down the line.

Summing Up

Paying attention to your income and expense cash flows is critical to your retirement happiness. You don't have to be controlled by the numbers, certainly, but if you want a comfortable standard of living, the ability to sleep at night without worrying about money, and to leave some funds to the kids, then watching your pennies will become second nature to you.

The trick to achieving a comfortable retirement lifestyle that you can sustain financially over the long haul is successful budgeting and regular monitoring. Living beyond your means may seem tempting for a while, but it cannot be maintained for any length of time, and it can have dire consequences. You need to learn to pace yourself financially by being aware of but not controlled by your financial limitations.

Top Ten Tips for Your Journey

1. If you have no idea how much you are spending in retirement, you will overspend.
2. If you overspend and overlive, you will run out of money but not out of years.
3. If you don't ask for discounts, you'll never get them.
4. Penny-pinching is simply "common cents."
5. Don't spend needlessly just to get loyalty points.
6. Never spend foolishly to impress friends or family.
7. Make every effort or sacrifice to protect your assets and avoid dipping into them to provide cash flow.
8. The items on your bucket list will change or perhaps be deleted as you grow older—don't be upset.
9. Seek part-time employment if you must, but do so for mental activity as much as financial need.
10. Think young, act your age … and spend frugally.

ESTATE PLANNING

CHAPTER 11

Peace of Mind as You Age

Each morning we are born again. What we do today matters most.
—Buddha

Up to this point we have talked about the work world and your new postwork life in somewhat idealistic terms. We have assumed, for example, that your time at work has enabled you to raise and launch your offspring into the world and that you are now free to do as you please. We have assumed that your dwelling is paid for, and your credit card debt is minimal. We have also assumed that you have oodles of free time to drive the grandkids around, and you enjoyed potty training so much with your own brood that you have volunteered to oversee this delightful task yet again.

Nice fantasy, wasn't it?

Unfortunately, in many cases the reality is that due to changed circumstances in your life or family needs, and perhaps due to the rising cost of everything from health care to day care, home care, groceries, and mortgage rates, you might well be at retirement age, but your household is anything but peaceful. Between caring for an aged parent with limited means, an ill spouse, an unemployed adult child who has returned home, or young grandchildren, in modern family life you can expect to address a variety of everyday issues—financial, medical, and legal matters, ranging from medical directives to making a will and inheritance issues.

The Sandwich Generation[39]

The phrase the *Sandwich Generation* was first coined by Dorothy Miller in 1981. The definition of the Sandwich Generation is being sandwiched between looking after an elderly parent and providing food and shelter and perhaps money to a stuck-at-home grown-up child.

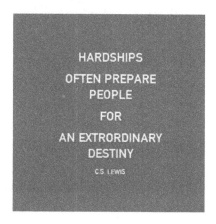

HARDSHIPS
OFTEN PREPARE
PEOPLE
FOR
AN EXTRORDINARY
DESTINY

C.S. LEWIS

According to PEW Research, "Nearly half (47%) of adults in their 40s and 50s have a parent age 65 or older and are simultaneously either raising a young child or financially supporting a grown child (age 18 or older)."[40] It is quite normal for people in these complex relationships to feel pulled in a number of directions, emotionally and financially, and the physical demands on their time can be quite exhausting, particularly when either their spouse or aged parent is unwell.

Interestingly, the trend toward caring financially for aged parents seems to be on the increase. The same study also revealed, "Adults under

39. Dorothy Miller, "The 'Sandwich' Generation: Adult Children of the Aging," Oxford Journals, Social Sciences, *British Journal of Social Work* 26, no. 5 (1981): 419–423.
40. "The Sandwich Generation, Rising Financial Burdens for Middle-Aged Americans," PEW Research, last modified January 30, 2013, http://www.pewsocialtrends.org/2013/01/30/the-sandwich-generation.

age 40 are the most likely to say an adult child has a responsibility to support an elderly parent in need. Eight-in-ten in this age group (81%) say this is a responsibility, compared with 75% of middle-aged adults and 68% of those ages 60 or older."[41] This might also be attributed to the fact that people over sixty are more likely to migrate from being the person providing assistance of some type to being the person in need of assistance with some aspect of their daily lives.[42]

In America, it is estimated that half of adults, age sixty or older, who have a living parent[43] say that the parent needs help with day-to-day living. This can manifest itself as anything from a drive to the mall, to arranging medical treatment, to overseeing household finances or providing emotional support. Even if you adore your parents, the dynamics of a once-harmonious family unit are strained equally for the adult support person and the elderly parent who is not used to being the one in need of assistance.

A Voice from the Past

This unaccustomed reliance on a relative, particularly an adult child, can be stressful for even close-knit families. Imagine the drama and discomfort that can ensue when circumstances force people who were estranged, for example, to suddenly have to interact with each other after years of silence, especially when the need for help commences without warning in the middle of the night due to an unexpected illness or injury.

You are fifty-five and struggling to keep your head above water at work, and you get a call to say that an aunt you have not seen in twenty years (and were never close to) is in the hospital in a city several hundred miles away. You, as her only relative, are going to have to fly there right away because the doctor won't agree to discharge the elderly aunt unless there is someone to care for her.

41. Ibid.

42. For people over the age of sixty who still have a living parent, the likelihood that the parent will need caregiving is relatively high.

43. "The Sandwich Generation, Rising Financial Burdens for Middle-Aged Americans," PEW Research, last modified January 30, 2013, http://www.pewsocialtrends.org/2013/01/30/the-sandwich-generation.

This is a no-win predicament for everyone. One minute the aged aunt is independently enjoying her life, and then—wham! Unexpectedly she falls and breaks a hip, and people she hasn't seen in ten years are summoned to her hospital room by well-intentioned social workers. Imagine the trauma of being forced to lie there while relatives she hasn't seen in years either stare in shameful silence or attempt to have a say regarding what's to be done with her. It is the moment that every person over the age of seventy dreads.

The emotional conflict created by this situation is extremely stressful and worrisome, whether we have the resources to spare or not. Most of us do not want to see an elderly person suffer, and so we put our lives on hold, and deal with the added emotional and financial responsibility as best we can. It can be very difficult to hold back feelings of resentment at being saddled with this burden if the person in need of assistance is also someone who was overly domineering, judgmental, or had outright banished you from his or her life.

If you find yourself in the middle of a predicament like this (whether you are the one in need of assistance or the would-be caregiver), do whatever it takes to put your personal feelings aside and deal with the facts of the situation until you can seek professional guidance or assistance. This can be a support group, parish priest, psychologist, family therapist, work-sponsored counseling program, or trusted family friend.

This is an any-port-in-the-storm situation, and there is no wrong way to seek objective support and guidance through this difficult time. The important thing is to avoid the assumption that you can or even should handle things alone. You may be perfectly justified in your hurt feelings, but this situation demands that you be objective, patient, and fair, whether the other person is or not. Keep in mind that while some fences cannot be mended overnight, this does not mean that it is not possible to patch things up with your wayward relations.

Life is a great deal easier when there is peace in the kingdom, and you chat once a week on the phone with your loved ones or get together for the occasional chicken dinner. It really doesn't matter what you talk about or whether you converse at all. Getting together to watch a movie, or listen to the news, or read the newspaper together in silence is better than not getting together at all. The point of these visits is human interaction, and this is both healthy and necessary for maintaining emotional well-being.

Making Your Wishes Known

So what should you talk about when you finally get tired of discussing the weather or the upcoming election? There is a laundry list of items that no one wants to talk about (or hear about) that really ought to be discussed while you are of sound mind and body. If you find mentioning any of the following is too difficult to contemplate, at least make up your mind what you would say if you could, and write it in a letter. Then show someone you trust where the letter is kept, and say, "If I am ever injured or unable to speak, please open this right away."

Obviously, this is the sort of letter that ideally should be prepared by a lawyer, and in truth, most jurisdictions require that the letter be drafted by a lawyer and witnessed in order for it to be legally binding. But if you can't afford a lawyer, many communities have some sort of legal aid organization that will assist you for free or at very low cost.

If using a lawyer is out of the question, go ahead and write the letter yourself. Even though there is no legal guarantee that your requests and instructions will be followed, at least the people who read the letter will be clear about what you would choose for yourself if you were able to converse. Please note this letter *is not* a will,[44] and it is *not* a medical power of attorney[45] and cannot be substituted for either. It is, at best, a *letter of wishes.*

This letter covers all the small things that others would wonder about if they had to suddenly care for you. It can contain anything from the security password for your Internet access to how many times a day your dog needs to be fed. There are no wrong things to put in your letter; the following are a few ideas to get you started:

---

44. A will is a legal document that tells what a person wants to have done with his or her assets (property, investments, chattels, and so forth) after his or her death.

45. A medical power of attorney is a legal instrument that allows you to select the person that you want to make health care decisions for you, if and when you become unable to make them for yourself.

- whom to contact if you are sick, including e-mail addresses and phone numbers
- how your monthly bills are paid and when they are due
- contact information for a pet sitter or kennel
- how often the sump pump needs to run
- where to find your will, medical directive, and power of attorney (if you have one)
- any prepaid final arrangements
- a complete, up-to-date list of all medications that you are taking
- a copy of your Do Not Resuscitate (DNR) order[46]
- any food or drug allergies
- a copy of your health insurance
- the location of any hidden object that you definitely want someone to find[47]
- the location of any safe deposit box and the contact information of anyone holding a spare key

Medical Directive

If you have dismissed the value of the above list because you already live with someone who knows all this information, move on to the next section (but it may not be a good idea to assume that the person knows all this). If you are sitting alone, wondering exactly what a medical directive is, the following may be of assistance:

A medical directive is a legal document that sets out how you wish to be treated *and* who is empowered to make decisions on your behalf for your medical treatment, if you are suddenly injured or incapacitated and cannot speak for yourself. It is also meant to empower someone to make

---

46. Do not resuscitate (DNR), or no code, is a legal order written either in the hospital or on a legal form to withhold cardiopulmonary resuscitation (CPR) or advanced cardiac life support (ACLS), in respect of the wishes of a patient in case his or her heart were to stop, or he or she were to stop breathing. This is typically obtained by terminally ill patients and the very elderly.

47. Older people frequently hide valuables and often forget where they put them. Just because you keep your diamonds in the flour canister or your priceless stamp collection in the wood pile, don't assume that anyone else will think to look there.

decisions in situations that you cannot predict. It can simply state who is in charge of making decisions regarding your health, or it can be very specific and outline how many weeks you wish to be left on life support if you are in a coma and it has been medically decided that you have no chance of waking up and making a recovery. Serious issues such as this may be predetermined by law or medical precedent, so ensure that proper advice is sought and followed.

It is understandable to not want to think about these things, but it is important for all older people to have some sort of medical instruction, and you may even find that it brings you and your family a certain peace of mind. Clearly, it should be drafted immediately if you have (or the person you live with has) been diagnosed with dementia, memory loss, or mental incapacitation or with a terminal illness, while it is still possible for the patient to make his or her wishes known.

Do Not Resuscitate (DNR)

At some point it may also be advisable for you or someone you are caring for to consider obtaining a Do Not Resuscitate (DNR) order. Many religions preach that it is a sin to interfere with the natural order of life, and we are respectful of that by not offering any opinions regarding this whatsoever. The following is simply a statement of the facts to assist you in your personal decision-making process.

Once upon a time, a critically ill, severely injured, or elderly person would reach the end of life and simply fall asleep and not wake up. The advances of medical science have changed all this, and it now possible to extend life for years and years, well beyond what was once possible, enabling people to spend time with their families and to make and enjoy the Third Journey.

There are even highly trained emergency services personnel who can be summoned to your bedside to provide lifesaving cardiopulmonary resuscitation (CPR) to get you through a health crisis. In many jurisdictions, the laws pertaining to lifesaving measures dictate that if the patient is unresponsive and cannot speak for himself (or herself) every effort should be made to resuscitate, regardless of the person's age or state of health. The assumption is quite literally that the patient would wish to keep living if it were possible to ask him or her; most of the time this will be the case.

There are times, however, at the latter stages of a terminal illness or prolonged suffering in extreme old age when this might not be what the patient wants at all. In some countries, in situations such as these, a DNR order, authorized and signed by a medical professional, can be presented to emergency services personnel to verify what, if any, medical treatment is desired. If you do not have a DNR (or if it is not presented when first responders arrive at the scene), emergency services is legally obliged to take aggressive measures to attempt to save your life, *even if your medical directive otherwise states that you do not wish aggressive measures be taken to extend your life.*

The law regarding these difficult subjects varies from one country to the next, and it is important to make sure you understand your rights as a patient in different medical situations in the country where you live so that you can make informed decisions for yourself and properly inform those around you of your wishes.

Power of Attorney

What happens to your finances if you become incapacitated?

As you get older, the chances of physical or mental problems unfortunately increase. Therefore, the possibility of your needing someone to look after your financial affairs becomes real.

- Whom do you trust?
- Do you have a family member you can trust?
- Do you have a friend you can trust?
- Should you go to a professional person, such as a lawyer?
- Should you set up something now?
- Should you wait until you develop an ailment?
- Can you secure your assets/liabilities/income and expenses watertight?

Obviously, you'd prefer not to upset or offend a family member (or a friend, if no family is available) by choosing one over another, especially if your finances are sizeable. Families can get awfully prickly about running Mom's or Dad's money, and it is not uncommon for suspicions to materialize—perhaps even accusations regarding the methods used by the entrusted person to do things right by you and, of course, do right for the rest of the family on your demise, in terms of your estate.

"I'm not saying you cheated, but you spent money on needless things."

One of the uglier aspects of handing over the affairs through a power of attorney is the possibility of mistreating the parent (in this case, you). Stories of elder abuse are far too common. Be aware that bank accounts, investment accounts, real estate, cars, boats, and jewelry are items that are susceptible to manipulation and sometimes outright expropriation, often without the knowledge of anyone else until it is too late.

There really is no way of planning in advance or even predicting that you will need someone to handle your money. Certainly, if you know in plenty of time that changes are taking place in your life or health that may render you unable to handle your finances alone, then make the right call early enough, while you are of sound mind and body.

Tricky, upsetting, but maybe it can't be avoided. Choose wisely.

Making a Will

It is equally important that you have a will prepared that meets all the legal requirements of the country in which you reside. In a few jurisdictions, it is permissible to purchase or download a will form off the Internet from a reputable source. This is a standard legal document with blank spaces for you to fill in regarding the disposition of your assets and to declare your beneficiaries. If you live in a country where this sort of document would hold up in court, make sure that you have it witnessed properly and that it meets the country's standards and requirements fully. In most cases, however, it is necessary to have your will prepared by a legal professional. There are often standard fees associated with this service, and it is quite all right to call up several law offices and ask what the fee would be for this service. Shop around.

Oddly enough, a lot of people put off making a will because they don't like thinking about the end. This is a rather naive but understandable fear that everyone should attempt to get over because the law varies widely from one jurisdiction to the next as to what happens if you die intestate (i.e., without a will). Some people do not think this matters because they don't possess a lot of property. But consider the following: would you really want a court or the government deciding what happens to your assets? How would you feel if they froze all your joint bank accounts, and your spouse was not able to buy groceries? Do you think it is fair to make grieving relatives plan and pay for your funeral if you have the means to organize and prepay these final expenses yourself?

These are blunt words on uncomfortable subjects, to be sure, but they are topics to which we recommend everyone should give some thought, even those in excellent health. Then make a calm, sensible plan; put it in motion; and go enjoy your life. True peace of mind can be that simple.

Case Study: *When is it okay to stay in your family homestead against your children's wishes?*

Bert and Joan live in northern England and have been married for over sixty years. They still live in their original family home, but their adult children have long since moved away.

Their daughter calls faithfully every Sunday, but the conversation is always the same: "Mum and Dad, you really need to be thinking about going into some sort of seniors home. I just hate thinking of you living in that drafty old house all by yourselves."

"Not a chance," Bert will say. "They'll carry me out in a box before I leave here."

No amount of argument or discussion will dissuade them from staying put.

Bert put it this way. "We have spent our whole lives in this house, and this is our home. We can still get out to the shops once a week, but if the time comes when I can't drive, we'll get a local taxi to come pick us up and bring us back. We don't buy much these days anyway. We eat well, we cook properly, and we have heat in the winter. So there's nothing we want for. If we need medical help, then local services send in a doctor or a nurse."

"So you are determined to maintain your independence?"

"I wouldn't say it like that," said Joan. "I would simply say that we are comfortable with each other. We look after each other, and if we were to go to a seniors home, we'd probably be separated. We don't want that. Dad's right. We'll stay here until the end."

"Well, why not come and live with us at our house?"

"Thanks, but no thanks," they both said. "We love you and the kids dearly, but we would feel we'd be a nuisance. You have your lives to live, and you don't want to be running after us all day. You both work, and we'd just be sitting in your house, watching TV, so why shouldn't we just watch it here?"

As much as their children think that they have their parents' best interests at heart, it is not possible for a younger person to fully appreciate what it is like to have lived so long that you find comfort in familiar surroundings and simply being together.

The moral is that if they are healthy enough, albeit a lot slower these days, and their mental functions are in good shape, then the decision to stay in their own home is a tough one to fight. They are living the life they choose, and who would challenge that?

If you are independent by nature and medically fit to live on your own, there is no reason to sell the family homestead before you are ready.

Inheritance Issues

The baby boomer generation still believes in setting their kids up for life, and if that means suffering financially to be able to leave a good level of finances for them, then some say it's fine. Fair enough, but be careful.

Some schools of thought, however, say that it's your money, it's your life, it's your choice, and therefore you should enjoy everything you worked hard for. Many people balk at the idea that they have to deny themselves certain things in order to leave their children money.

Obviously, if you have so much money that you can both enjoy yourself to the fullest *and* still leave plenty when you depart, then you're really in great shape.

Of course, there are many places you can leave your money apart from the family—charities, hospitals, public television, libraries, universities, and so forth. These places are all very grateful for financial support, and they certainly provide an alternative to family squabbling.

Considerable emotion is attached to the inheritance issue. It is not fun to have a real discussion regarding the time when you and/or your spouse will not be around. And even if you want to have this discussion, you may encounter family members who flat out refuse to discuss your mortality. With that in mind, you must make every effort to make sure that your wishes are known and arrangements are in place for these wishes to be implemented.

Most families will make it clear to the parents that the money is not an important issue. Most children will demand that their parents live an enjoyable and financially secure retirement.

The complexities associated with inheritance issues are that your kids likely won't know how much you will leave to them on death. You may not even be fully aware yourself. Then the differentiation between liquid and nonliquid assets comes into play. If you own your own home, it will have a value, but will not be a cash asset unless the children sell it on your passing. It is always a good idea to work out in advance how that asset gets split on liquidation between the family members. In other words, you make the decision, rather than them.

During your lifetime, apart from the obvious benefit of having a place to stay, the house is not a contributing asset to your cost of living cash needs, so selling it in advance doesn't help you in your retirement (unless you need the cash). You want the property to be distributed on death, not before. Therefore, there is no pressure to liquidate that asset while you are still here, just for inheritance purposes. Tax consequences may be an integral part of this issue.

Typically, most of your other assets are financial assets (e.g., residual balances on pension schemes, investment portfolios, and life insurances). Once again, unless you need the cash earlier, there is no need to liquidate any of them prior to death. But again, it is wise to set out, through a will or letter of wishes, precisely how you want them to be distributed.

Due to the emotional issues and the legal issues, you should give very serious consideration to this topic, and discuss it with your legal representative, who will not only advise on the legal matters but also will do so in an impartial, unemotional, professional manner.

Taking the "let them sort it out when I'm gone" approach is really *not* the best plan.

Elder Abuse

And now we will discuss the one topic we should not have to include at all—elder abuse.

There are still some countries where elders are viewed with the utmost respect and consideration, and families pull together to care for their aging relatives without hesitation. Unfortunately, the Western world is going through a dark phase where this is not necessarily the case. In the United States, elder abuse is defined as "any knowing, intentional, or negligent act by a caregiver or any other person that causes harm or a serious risk of harm to a vulnerable adult."[48] The abusers can be male or female, health care workers, family members, or trusted friends. This crime (and yes, it is a *crime*) often goes unreported because the elderly person is dependent upon the abuser for the necessities of life and either doesn't know his or her rights or is too afraid to speak up.

The following is a list of the most common types of abuse. The perpetrators are often motivated by greed or a need to dominate or assume power over another human being.[49] The legal definitions and classifications of abuse vary from one jurisdiction to the next, but in general, the following may be used as a guide:

- *physical abuse*—inflicting physical pain or injury on a senior (e.g., slapping, bruising, or restraining by physical or chemical means)
- *sexual abuse*—nonconsensual sexual contact of any kind

48. "What is Elder Abuse?" Administration on Aging, last modified July 22, 2016, http://www.aoa.gov/aoa_programs/elder_rights/ea_prevention/whatisea.aspx.
49. Ibid.

- *neglect*—the failure by those responsible to provide food, shelter, health care, or protection for a vulnerable elder
- *exploitation*—the illegal taking, misuse, or concealment of funds, property, or assets of a senior for someone else's benefit
- *emotional abuse*—inflicting mental pain, anguish, or distress on an elder person through verbal or nonverbal acts (e.g., humiliating, intimidating, or threatening)
- *abandonment*—desertion of a vulnerable elder by anyone who has assumed the responsibility for care or custody of that person
- *self-neglect*—the failure of a person to perform essential self-care tasks and that such failure threatens his/her own health or safety

If you are being subjected to some form of abuse (or you suspect that someone you know is being abused), do *not* be afraid or embarrassed to report it. Many people find it hard to believe that what they are experiencing is really abuse because there is such a stigma attached to this term, but they know when something that is happening to them is not right and causing them stress. You can talk to your doctor, your parish priest, or any form of social services hotline that exists in your area. There is no shame in wanting to live a safe, peaceful life. You are entitled to this, even if you are no longer able to care for yourself without assistance. Find the courage to tell someone if you need help.

Many of the issues mentioned in this chapter are extremely sensitive and for many, awkward to discuss. As such, objective and sensible thought by all parties must be implemented at some point. It is possible that you will sail through the rest of your life without any need to pay attention to some of these matters. However, in most cases, one or more situations will arise or should be raised, where the matter must be taken care of. It is far better to address these matters, such as your will, well in advance of a time when you have no option but to think about it, when your mind may be focused on other more pressing concerns, such as a medical problem. Early attention to these life-critical issues, including professional advice where necessary, will make the final days easier to navigate for all concerned.

Top Ten Tips for Your Journey

1. The Sandwich Generation factor will challenge you to look at your life and your family in new ways.
2. The secret to juggling competing priorities is to stay calm.
3. Everyone deserves to live and die with dignity.
4. Draft a letter of wishes—"this is what I want or need if something incapacitating happens to me."
5. Draft a medical directive in the event of a serious health issue.
6. A will is a legal document and should be prepared properly.
7. The will should alleviate family squabbles after your passing.
8. Elder abuse is a serious matter. Don't be afraid to speak up if you are the victim.
9. Do not help someone else abuse an elderly person by staying silent.
10. Serious matters in life should be treated seriously.

QUALITY OF LIFE

Managing Long-Term Relationships

There are many personal long-term relationships in life, both in the traditional and nontraditional family structure, such as civil marriage, common law marriage, life partners, friends, roommates, companions, and acquaintances. As these relationships evolve over time, changes inevitably take place, perhaps the most significant of which is when one or both parties enter their Third Journey. The impact of being home all day, possibly for the first time in many years, may cause significant turbulence in the relationship.

We openly acknowledge that there are lots of people who are quite happy to be home together, and their bonds of friendship and companionship just continue to improve over time. Most of the following information is offered in an effort to assist those who are struggling with this new experience of constant togetherness. For this discussion, we will assume that the relationship has been in existence for a good number of years and that both partners have reasonably good health.

Long-term relationships are multifaceted and include: emotional, mental, physical, psychological, and sexual considerations. However, human nature being what it is, the interplay of psychology between the two individuals tends to overshadow and increasingly control all of their interactions as they age. Even simple things, such as balancing the checkbook, visiting the grandkids, home improvements, who will drive, which groceries to buy, where to go on vacation, and which friends to invite over for dinner can cause friction. Without proper management, these relationships can disintegrate to the point that there is little cooperation between the two parties, and every interaction is approached as if it was a battle to be won or lost.

The Albatross at the Breakfast Table

Typically, one or both partners have been substantially out of the house during the workweek for many years. That lifestyle allowed each partner to independently establish an identity, build a self-focused (not necessarily self-centered) life, and populate it with their own friends. As such, the time spent together has been confined to evenings, weekends, and vacations. Depending on the stress of the workweek, even these free periods were largely taken up with the "get home, eat, television, bed" pattern, thus leaving little time for true bonding. Often, even if there is an issue to discuss, tiredness and a reluctance to endure another one of "those conversations" can have an impact on the quality of the conversation.

This pattern, over time, becomes the habit and, generally speaking, most people will accept it as part of a normal long-term relationship. It becomes routine.

Then, wham—retirement comes along, and you wake up sitting at the breakfast table with a person you barely know anymore. Count yourself lucky if you are simply confronted with long patches of awkward silence, but it doesn't usually go that way.

If both partners' retirement dates approximately coincide, then the wham is a big wham, but it isn't necessarily any better if one partner retires ahead of the other; then they actually have to make two adjustments— first to being home alone all day, and then to having too much company when his or her life partner is suddenly home all day as well, just when the first person had adjusted to being alone.

Emotionalism Rules the Day

Living together under the same roof was fine in the working years, but now the household dynamic has changed, radically and permanently.

Bumping into each other in the kitchen several times a day, refusing to share the TV remote, interrupting the washing sequence, to-ing and fro-ing with endless cups of coffee, going to help (or hinder) with the grocery shopping, using all the hot water for endless showers, and so forth. It is not uncommon to discover that one person in the relationship is seeking more togetherness than the other one, who is seeking more space. This is a no-win scenario for both people, as the more one person clings onto the other one, the more that person pulls away, and vice versa.

We have not been accustomed to having another person around all day, regardless of the romantic connection—and we can't easily ignore the person when we become fed up with constant togetherness. Tensions rise, and little things start to annoy and perhaps even stress you out. Leaving the top off the ketchup bottle can start a new family feud—matters that were totally irrelevant and usually ignored when you were working and out of the house. Now the slightest little aggravation can descend into verbal abuse, both ways.

There is no doubt that being at home together all day, every day, will test the best of relationships. It is simply human nature and not uncommon at all. Chances are that the physical romance (sex, if you prefer) in the marriage may have dissipated a long time ago (if not, good for you, and enjoy), so there is no chance of a denial of conjugal rights as a revenge tactic through a falling out over the ketchup. Therefore, other retributions are usually found.

Some couples seem to delight in the mental warfare, not talking to each other for hours or days on end, storming out of the house without telling their partners where they are going or when they will be back, and trying to get their adult children to take sides.

A report titled "Who Will Love Me When I'm 64?" jointly published by Relate Charity (UK) and the New Philanthropy Capital suggests there are changes in the nature of relationships of elderly couples today, compared with the previous generation.

Divorce rates of men and women over sixty increased between 1991 and 2011, it notes, whereas those of younger couples have fallen in the past ten years.

It pointed out that baby boomers, defined as those born between 1946 and 1964 (today's pensioners) had "married young and in great numbers." But "they were far more likely to divorce than their parents."

The truth is that unless couples find ways to adequately develop and manage a brand-new relationship between husband and wife, it is highly possible that life in the old homestead will never be the same again. Given that this can be the reality for the rest of your respective lives, it is a critically important issue to recognize—and get sorted out.

So what's the answer?

Time Together and Time Apart

The solution to maintaining a happy and peaceful home life in retirement is to realize that the person sitting across from you is struggling just as much as you are (for completely different reasons that you may never fully understand). Commit to taking this transition slowly. Be patient with your partner and yourself, and develop some interests outside the home. While being online most of the day means that you can sit on your sofa and surf the world, there is still a great need for human interaction—interaction beyond just your life partner.

In another part of this book, we discuss hobbies, part-time work, volunteering, charity work, and so forth. Having outside interests keeps the mind active and provides opportunities to keep up with what is going on in the community. Find a way to make a contribution or travel to the destinations you fancy.

If both partners have the same interests and can jointly enjoy them, then fine. If you have diverse interests, however, then those interests must be followed individually, and each partner must accept that some things will be done alone. Holding back a partner from doing what he or she wants and needs to do in his or her Third Journey will have long-term damaging effects on the relationship. Within reason, each partner should unreservedly accept the other partner's wishes.

Everyone needs his or her own space. Whether he has his den or "man room," and she has her office or knitting room, individual space becomes a protected sanctuary in the home. Entry into the other partner's space can be a provocative move that can lead to open hostility. "Stuff" in the space is treated as very private and personal. The belongings in the space likely are not embarrassing by nature, but they are his (or hers) and must be protected.

Invasion by other family members, especially if frequent, can be a challenge. "Oh no, here come the grandkids [or your brother, or cousin, or …] again!" he says, while the wife loves the attention. He sees it as a distraction from his peace and quiet. She sees it as a distraction from him.

This probably is a man versus woman issue, in that he loves the grandkids for sure but can only take their frenetic energy in small doses. His wife, however, craves more and more time with them. It shouldn't be a challenging situation, providing both husband and wife understand each other's feelings and respect those feelings fully. Using the grandkids (or any other family member) as a means of annoying the other is a foolproof way to ensure that the husband/wife relationship will be on shaky ground. Discussion, appreciation, and negotiation must take place.

The Romantic Side of Things

Every psychologist or professional advisor will say that a good sex life is the cornerstone of a long-lasting relationship. Maybe so. But if the desire disappeared several years ago during the working years—through tiredness, poor circulation, low testosterone, low estrogen, no time, or just no interest anymore—it may take a seismic shift in libido to rekindle it now in the retirement years.[50] That is a fact in most cases, not just an observation.

Regardless that some lifestyle gurus try to make us feel inferior if we are not jumping in the sack five times a week when we are sixty-nine, the reality is, most of us don't. Yes, some couples do manage to maintain an active sexual relationship, but you must not feel inadequate if you don't have the interest nowadays. There's nothing wrong with you or your partner. It happens to most of us. It makes no difference whether it is biological, or emotional, or we just can't perform like we did years ago. If the physical part of the romance has melted away, so be it. You can feel guilty if you wish, and you can feel that you are not satisfying your

---

50. If both partners do want to embark on a quest for their missing sex life, the Third Journey is the perfect time to rekindle and explore their intimate relationship. Talking to your health care professional or reading one of the many books available on the subject is a great way to start.

partner if you wish, but if it "ain't gonna happen, it ain't gonna happen." Get over it, and find a way to be friends who cuddle. Enjoy every other part of your lives together.

The notion that love can only be present if there is sex is nonsense. Love can migrate into just caring for each other and respecting each other's wishes. The occasional holding hands or a hug and kiss at night is perfectly reasonable. The longer you live with a person, the more you know that person. Therefore, know what he or she wants and likes and respond accordingly. That is just as much love as physical romping, certainly in these latter years. Psychological intimacy is equally as important as physical intimacy as we age.

Lastly, every effort should be made to keep up your appearance and look good for the sake of your own self-esteem and for your partner. The idea that you can eat whatever you want and ignore your waistline may be deemed a reward for getting this far in life, but apart from the obvious health consequences, if you let yourself go, you really can't complain that your partner has decided to do the same. You may not feel the need to dress up all the time, but now and again, if you go out to dinner or a party or a family event, dressing nicely should be a big part of sustaining your long-term relationship. Look good, feel good, be good.

Enjoying Time Together

One of the comments many people make about the Third Journey is that this is the time to enjoy doing "what I want to do." In many respects, that is a fair statement. After all, you can argue that you worked hard all your life, probably for someone else, so it's now your turn to do it for yourself.

Obviously, this can cause some friction in long-term relationships. If both husband and wife want to do exactly the same things in life (e.g., cruising, hill-walking, volunteering, playing golf, gardening, and so forth), then all will be fine. However, if one partner feels the need to do something or go someplace that the other partner has no interest in, every effort must be made to accept this decision without resentment.

If the decision is to go away from home for a period of time, long or short, and do something that only *you* fancy doing (and it is financially feasible without putting undo strain on the budget), then your spouse should do his or her best to agree to your doing it. Obviously, if you run the family finances, and being away from home might cause disruption to checking accounts, bill paying, and the like, then you need to make all the necessary arrangements before leaving. And of course, you should be able to be contacted in the event of an emergency.

Sometimes in retirement you can be faced with a burning desire to go on a journey that is of no interest to your partner. If this notion won't go away, make every effort to make a short trip (even if it is simply to spend a little time finding yourself). The idea that one partner needs time away from the other partner can cause upset and confusion, but, especially in these latter years, being away for a short while should be encouraged and embraced. Chances are that when you return home, you will discover that the time apart did you both some good.

Caregiving

At the start of this chapter we assumed that both partners were in good health, albeit you are both aging. Each partner should make every effort to eat properly, exercise if possible, sleep properly, take all prescriptions correctly, and have regular medical checkups. However, if an illness materializes, especially if it is chronic and life-threatening, count on your relationship changing in ways you would never have imagined. It can be a time to rekindle a close, loving bond or to become completely estranged. Don't assume that your spouse won't support you and doesn't understand what you are going through just because you have not been close lately. It is not uncommon for a relationship that may have drifted apart, especially in the retirement years, to come back together again when one partner is called upon to care for the other.

One of the health-related problems of aging, apart from the medical condition itself, is the loss of independence and self-respect. If you get to the stage in life when you are infirm and not very mobile, then personal functions, such as bathing and grooming, can become awkward, if not impossible. You may have to rely on your partner to help with the most personal of daily functions.

Case Study: *How important is it for a caregiver to also take care of himself or herself?*

Dan lives in London and retired almost three years ago. His wife of over forty years retired two years before him. When he was home all day, their relationship was generally good. They each did their own thing during the day, but made a point of coming together for the evening meal, if not before. They had discussed going on vacations together when retired and have done a few trips, mostly weekenders into Europe.

Tragically, about two years ago, his wife was diagnosed with a degenerative illness, which became a terminal illness. As it progressed, her approach to life was fairly upbeat, but most days she wasn't cognizant of problems in the house or family. Dan covered for her.

He said, "Some days she will watch TV all day and be very happy, while I do the cooking and cleaning. I don't really have an issue with that, although I would welcome some help. I've tried to discuss her condition with her in real terms, not medical, but I get nowhere. We have decisions to make about taking care of her as we move along and whether I am capable to do that. We've loosely talked about moving to a place where the family could help, but again the conversation is short-lived. I could make the decisions myself alone, but that's not fair.

"Everyone advises me to take a break for a few days to recharge my batteries, but I would feel incredibly guilty leaving my wife with anyone else. On a bad day, she panics if I leave her for longer than it takes to do the grocery shopping.

"I've been to counselors and medical psychologists and so forth. They are all supportive, of course, but until they live this kind of life themselves, they have no deep feelings of the emotions I'm suffering every day and night. There is absolutely no question that the relationship between my wife and me has deteriorated enormously over this past year in particular."

Dan is not alone with this type of dilemma. His own health is suffering through not eating, not sleeping, and not being able to get out of the house much, and thus he ends up day after day in the claustrophobic atmosphere of a relationship that has no happy ending.

It is critically important for a caregiver to learn how to adequately care for himself (or herself) at the same time that he is tending to the needs of the spouse.

Hopefully, your relationship is strong enough to accept the help of your partner as needed and realize that you still have a much-needed role to play in his or her life. An illness and/or some form of disability can bring partners closer together or, unfortunately, push them further apart. Both scenarios are possible; and it really comes down to your own personal circumstances. Hopefully, you will be there for each other, both in the good times and the bad times. If you both agree that improvement is needed, and you seem to be at an impasse, don't forget that you can always buy a relationship workbook, attend a couples workshop, or seek the guidance of a marriage counselor to repair your relationship at any point along the way.

When the Walls Come Tumbling Down

One of the sadder facts of getting older is that you may well outlive your life partner. The impact on the person who is left is considerable, and the consequential cycle of grief and recovery should not be underestimated. Similarly, you may well find yourself alone as a result of divorce or a medically necessitated separation when your spouse requires more medical attention than you are able to provide at home.

All these gut-wrenching situations typically cause at least temporary apathy, loss of appetite, stress, and sleeplessness that can lead to depression and chronic illness if not managed properly. Each situation has its own cycles of mourning and recovery, and these are really beyond the scope of this book. If you find yourself in any one of these situations, please seek support and counseling to assist with your adjustment to your new circumstances.

Rebuilding Your Life

Regardless of how it came about, there is usually little joy in finding independence at this age. It is a slow uphill struggle to regain your sense of balance and perspective, but it is a journey you must make if you are going to thrive. You must choose either to learn to be happy flying solo or to be open to the idea of meeting another person to spend your remaining years with. In this modern age, this can be anything from someone you have lunch with on Sundays to a full-blown love affair.

Admittedly, the thought of starting a new relationship can be too much to bear for many people. In some cases, they just can't be bothered— or they could be bothered, but the fear of being left alone *again* a few years from now prevents them from making the effort. Remarriage just doesn't seem plausible to many. Yet those who do remarry often find a new and lasting peace of mind because they bring a sense of wisdom and perspective to the relationship that they perhaps did not possess in their youth. The companionship is probably the uppermost reason for seeking a new partner, and that alone is a strong reason to contemplate taking the plunge again. If it happens, and you get pleasure from doing it, then good for you. Your final days will be happy ones.

Other Relationships

Apart from the long-term relationship between husband and wife, there are also many other relationships that can change in the latter years.

The relationship between you and your children and grandchildren is one of the most evident and most important. Now that Grandpa is at home all day, is that a good thing or a bad thing?

Babysitting and driving grandkids back and forth to school, soccer practice, the dentist, the doctor, or birthday parties sounds like fun to some folks but can be seen as being used if you are expected to care for them at night while your adult children go clubbing. The trade-off of showing affection for the grandkids and the sense of duty to look after them more, now that you are retired, is finely balanced against the feeling of being played on by the grandkids' parents. It can cause friction and resentment. Do not be afraid to set reasonable boundaries regarding when you are available, what you will do, and what you will pay for.

Families should recognize that this is your time to enjoy yourself and not simply view you as an old chauffeur or babysitter. Helping out now and again is fine, but perpetual running after the grandkids because the parents are working or out enjoying themselves should be curtailed. The kids will be at this growing-up stage of their life for several years, and for every year they grow and get older, *so do you*. It is important to pace yourself so you can have the energy to be a positive force in their lives for years to come.

One of the primary reasons that older folks try their best to not upset the status quo is the realization that in a few years' time they may very well need the family to look after them. It's all very well to demand your own space and time now, when your health is in good shape, but if you don't make yourself available at all, there is always the possibility that when you need your children due to failing health, they may just turn away from you. The old structure of the family taking care of the old folks is not as strong in most societies these days. You need to maintain some sort of an ongoing relationship with the people that you are counting on to see you through the rest of your life.

In conclusion, never lose sight of the fact that your relationships have both a physical and a psychological aspect. You cannot live in harmony unless both components are in balance. Your relationships will continue to evolve and change throughout your Third Journey. There is a temptation to become complacent, but your long-term emotional well-being depends on your ability to learn to work together *and* to give each other space to breathe as you age.

Top Ten Tips for Your Journey

1. Everyone has relationships in their lives.
2. Everyone has the option to choose which ones they want.

3. Relationships require a give-and-take approach—the less you give, the less you can expect in return.
4. Long-term relationships stay long due to mutual respect and, more important, due to an attitude of "live and let live."
5. If fighting over the TV remote is an issue, get another TV.
6. Find things to do in the home that improve your living standards.
7. Find things to do outside the home that improve your state of mind.
8. As we age, sex becomes of less interest (and probably is less doable)—so be it.
9. Brush your hair whether you are staying home today or going out to meet the local mayor. Look after your appearance.
10. Think young, but act your age.

CHAPTER 13

Overcoming Loneliness in the Third Journey

In this chapter we will discuss the challenges of overcoming loneliness.

In retirement we know that we must stay active. Some of us may even feel we want to be productive. But if the underlying cause for concern and unhappiness stems from being alone, then we must put extra effort into redefining our lifestyles. It won't get fixed all by itself through time or healing.

In other parts of this book, we addressed the emotional impact—the psychomotivation, as we call it—of the events in a person's life and how these events can cause serious concerns and stress. Humans are highly social beings, and as much as it is normal to not want to think about stressful events, we do tend to assume that if we ever find ourselves in a predicament, there would be someone there to assist with the problem at hand or at the very least to listen to our concerns. It is pretty much inconceivable for us to believe that we might not have someone to lean on.

However, the longer we live, the more likely it is that we will arrive at a point where it appears that we do not have anyone familiar to lean on.

Finding Yourself Alone

Very few people plan to wind up alone. Sometimes it happens suddenly due to divorce or the death of a life partner, and sometimes it happens so gradually as family move away and lifelong friends pass away that it is almost a shock to realize there is no one left. In either case, the worst part of this predicament is the moment that we realize that although we might have prepared ourselves for the idea of living alone, we are utterly unprepared for the overwhelming, debilitating sense of loneliness that tags along with it.

Regardless of the circumstances, loneliness is one of the few universal challenges of Oldsters today. It is no exaggeration to opine that in the case of severe loneliness, the person might easily prefer death—a strong and morbid statement perhaps, but loneliness is a cancer of the psyche that can eat away at the person's will to live, making all life seem futile and ultimately causing the mind to seek relief in any shape or form.

The Effects of Loneliness

Probably the first and perhaps foremost emotional impact is the *loss of companionship.*

Having someone in the house provides an outlet for chat, for complaints, for excitement, for arguing, and for commiserating to the point that the person's mere presence is a comfort that we frequently take for granted.

Certainly as we get older and if we have been in the same house with a partner for a long time, emotions and feelings can get all mixed up. Sometimes our partners are our best friends; sometimes we simply can't stand their presence, much less their opinions, and we thrive on the unending controversy. We get angry, we get short, we get frustrated, and we take it out on the other person, either through argument or silence.

Then, something happens, and that person is no longer around.

No one to talk to; no one to moan to; no one to ask for advice or help; no one to lend a hand with the groceries; no one to hold; no one to watch a movie with; no one to eat dinner with; no one to go to bed with. No one.

The emptiness is gut-wrenching, so much so that it is not uncommon to romanticize the memory of what you had and see it through rose-colored glasses, to the point that even a truly bad marriage can be pined for.

From a psychological perspective, loneliness can trigger feelings of despair and isolation that can lead to prolonged depression. It may start as sadness when the loved one departs (which is a completely normal part of the grieving process), but left unchecked, it can turn into self-pity, frustration, and anger, culminating in a depression syndrome. Clearly, issues of a medical nature (chronic illness, for example), financial distress, or family upheaval can and do cause stress, anxiety, and then depression, but the loneliness factor is very high on that list.

Countless numbers of men and women live on their own. Some thrive, depending on their temperament and the true nature of the relationship from which they have been released. Some Oldsters have so much fun with this newfound freedom that they bounce from one project to another with glee and sheer satisfaction. It certainly can be a rewarding time and perhaps a lifestyle that they have craved for years but were stuck in a relationship that didn't provide that excitement. If you are blessed to be better off on your own than you were in a relationship, do not be afraid to embrace your good fortune—there is nothing for you to feel regretful about. Get out of bed each day and enjoy your revitalized Third Journey.

On the other hand, if loneliness is an issue for you, and you see no way out, then you must do everything possible to fight against the slippery slope leading to despair and medical depression.

It is a fact that as we age we do get more frail and more sensitive. We also get more upset and indeed frightened by the smallest event. An unexpected knock at the door, or a strange phone call at a strange time can cause panic. The electricity in the house goes out. And if there is no one else in the house to converse with, the feeling of despair and helplessness is all too evident.

Symptoms of Loneliness

There any many symptoms of loneliness leading to depression:

- a general feeling of sadness or feeling down
- a lack of interest in normal lifestyle and activity

- inability to find pleasure in normal high-interest events
- changes in sleep patterns—poor sleep, irregular sleep, or significant insomnia
- a feeling of wanting to sleep all the time or at unusual times of the day
- difficulty getting out of bed in the morning
- reduced interest in family members or activities
- withdrawal symptoms from daily interests and responsibilities
- denial of feelings of depression to friends and family
- an unusual or sudden loss of weight
- a loss of focus on everyday interests, reduced concentration, and indecisiveness
- unusual health complaints—sore limbs, sore eyes, headaches, backache
- memory problems
- digestive system upset
- increased emotions of loneliness
- feeling abnormally self-critical
- feeling of not being in control, feeling overwhelmed
- feeling miserable all the time
- reduced or complete loss of self-esteem or self-worth
- a feeling of unusual tiredness, exhaustion, or irritability
- changes in normal eating routines—eating too much or poor food, or loss of appetite
- excessive mood swings, ranging from irritability to high levels of excitement

Yet perhaps the most acute psychological impact is the feeling of "This will never change. I will feel like this and be on my own for the rest of my life." The depth of despair cannot be appreciated by those who are with a partner. It is one thing to recognize that loneliness is a very sad experience, but it is quite something else to actually be in that situation and have to face it every minute of every day.

Making Changes to Your Situation

First and foremost, it is critically important to recognize that being alone is an opportunity to get reacquainted with yourself. Some people who find themselves living on their own unexpectedly are highly resistant to this idea, but the fact remains that while you were in a long-term relationship, you were focusing a lot of time and energy on someone else, and chances are you were so absorbed in meeting someone else's needs that you forgot what sort of things you truly enjoy.

Second, if you have spent a long time in a relationship, whether that relationship was generally happy or not, that relationship is the only way of being that you know. Before you can consider whether or not you want to remain alone or meet someone new, you need to take some time to breathe. The number one task right now is to learn who you really are at this point in your life and learn to like that person. It is not realistic to think that you will meet someone new and form a lasting bond unless you first are willing to be true to yourself.

This does not mean that you need to stay home; it is important for you to be out and about as soon as possible. But it does mean that it is a good idea not to rush into any big commitments simply to avoid being alone. The best thing to do, until you start feeling better, is simply keep busy.

The following ideas will get you started:

1. Get out and about in the community. Join social clubs or visit libraries or museums. Go have coffee at the mall regularly. Merely watching people whiz by, even though they have no connection to you, will help.

2. Join Facebook groups and/or chat rooms. Be very, very careful, of course, and only join reputable groups—and be ultra-careful about giving personal details, such as e-mail addresses, credit card numbers, and so forth. You can observe a group without joining it to determine whether it is right for you, and once you join, you can still leave the group permanently if anything makes you the slightest bit uncomfortable. Having said this, if you take your time to find the right group for you, these groups can be a

great source of friendship and fellowship. Even though you may never meet the people in person, you know they are there for you. They probably are lonely like you and most are willing to chat. Try things such as Skype as well.

3. Obviously, your church and its activities can be a wonderful place to be part of the crowd. Get involved with activities that you've never done before. Be bold. Get on the stage and do the Nativity play. Act as DJ at the next barn dance.

4. Get a pet. Dogs, in particular, are simply marvelous companions. They are obedient (hopefully), don't speak back, need to be fed by you, and their most favorite thing to do in the world is whatever you are doing right now. You will get attached to your pooch, and it can be a tremendous experience, every day, all day, for both of you.

5. Volunteer to assist any charity in your area. It will get you out of the house and help you make a few new friends, not to mention that you will be doing your part to help the people in your community.

6. Join a walking club (or start one in your neighborhood). There is nothing like a good brisk walk to chase the blues away, and the exercise will do you good.

7. Establish a daily routine composed of a mixture of activities, and stick to it until things get easier. Simply knowing what you are going to do next throughout the day will help you stay positive.

Case Study: *Is loneliness really that big a problem for Oldsters in the Internet age?*

Elsa lives alone in a remote part of the Philippines. She lost her husband over ten years ago and has been on her own ever since. Her family left home many years ago and live a fair distance away from her, so visiting is not a regular occurrence.

When she was younger, she never minded being alone and was an active member of her church. Now that she is not able to get around as easily as she used to, she is beginning to feel isolated. She still sees her friends on Sundays but spends many days at home, looking at four walls. "I have a small garden, but I get tired of that quickly these days. I never watched much TV, so that doesn't help," she says.

However, one thing Elsa does have, which is the difference between loneliness and utter despair, is her Internet connection to the outside world.

Loneliness is one of the worst ailments in the older years. Having no one to converse with day after day after day will lead even the most rational person to boredom, despondency, and eventually depression. One of the most widespread "illnesses" in today's retirement communities is loneliness.

Elsa, fortunately, has two cats that share her house with her. "They must be the most educated cats in the world," she says. "I talk to them all the time. They are as politically current as most politicians around these parts. I read to them from online newspapers and so forth. The nice thing is that they don't ever argue with me."

Elsa admits that there have been moments when she was tempted to think of her good health as a burden. "What's the point in living until I'm in my nineties to simply lead this debilitating existence?" she asks.

The trauma of loneliness is one of those lifestyle problems that, until it is experienced personally, is often ignored by society and certainly by family. A simple phone call or an e-mail might add some purpose to the person's life. Too often, the lonely person simply turns into a kind of hermit until he or she eventually fades away. For society, that may be an acceptable path to follow, but for the person suffering the loneliness, his or her usefulness is severely tested every day.

"I still enjoy cooking," Elsa says, "but I am not as experimental as I used to be. I feed the cats and then myself, and then I chat with my friends online for the rest of the day. I was never tech savvy, but I persevered in learning how to use a computer, and then I joined Facebook, and the world opened up to me."

Being confined in your house most of the day, perhaps every day, without any human contact is not good for you. Particularly if you live in an urban area, you simply must get yourself out the door as often as possible. It does not do to sit in a dark corner while the world rushes by just a few feet away, especially when there are thousands of other people around you who are in the same predicament. Make it your business to find out when and where other people on their own meet up, and go join them. You may never replace the person you lost, but you will definitely have things in common to discuss with others.

The Third Journey is a wonderful time to get up, get moving, and get your life back. Good luck.

Top Ten Tips for Your Journey

1. The words "being alone" and "loneliness" have different meanings.
2. Getting older and becoming lonely are normal, natural events.
3. The loss of companionship in the home should be replaced outside the home.
4. Don't be afraid to seek intimacy in a new relationship.
5. If your sexual performance has diminished, relax; you can still enjoy closeness.
6. Turn your loneliness into a freedom trail, and plan self-enjoyment.
7. If you wake up in the middle of the night and feel lonely, make coffee.
8. The feeling of loneliness may not last your lifetime; events can happen to change it.
9. Find activities in your community, and overcome your shyness. Join in.
10. Eat properly, stay healthy, keep fit, and maintain your energy levels.

CHAPTER 14

The Function of Self-Regeneration

The time has come, the Walrus said, to talk of many things: of
shoes—and ships—and sealing wax—of cabbages—and kings.
—Lewis Carroll, *Through the Looking Glass*

Just as you might decide to renovate an outdated house, when you pass through the retirement threshold, you arrive at a point where you have the opportunity to renovate your lifestyle. We call this process *self-regeneration*[51] because it is a self-directed, self-controlled, multistep project in which you work on the parts of yourself (including your mental, emotional, spiritual, physical, and psychological self) that time or circumstances have prevented you from developing as completely as you would have liked in your earlier years. There is no time like the present to make the changes that could and should be made.

When we advocate self-regeneration, we are not suggesting that you are not fully formed; that would be absurd. You have reached an age

---

51. For the purpose of this discussion, we define self-regeneration not as self-initiated growth but as self-initiated striving to grow. "Not everyone who tries to grow more mature in body, psyche, or spirit actually does grow. Equally we acknowledge that some people who aren't trying to grow may actually do so as a result of events taking place in their lives, or even divine intervention."—Dr. Bob Ritzema, Olderhood team psychologist.

when you know what you want, and you know what you like. You also know what you do not like, and you are usually pretty quick to dismiss anything that is of no interest. We won't waste time trying to tell you what you need to do. We will simply start by asking that you consider whether there are any aspects of your younger self that have slipped into disuse, that you would like to restore or reactivate.

Think of this as a time to recall some of the more adventurous bits of yourself from the days when you were fearless enough to ask a girl on a date, carefree enough to backpack across Europe, or determined enough to stand in line all night long to buy concert tickets. If you have never done any of these things, and you are blissfully rocking away on the back porch, close this book and walk away. No one is going to try to make you do anything you really don't want to do. You should at least be aware, however, that you don't have to sit out the rest of your life on the sidelines if you would rather be busy and having new experiences.

If, on the other hand, you have run out of closets to sort, have hovered over your spouse until he or she stopped speaking to you, are sick of pacing in circles in the living room, and have so much pent-up energy that you can't sit still, perhaps we can make a few suggestions that you might find beneficial.

Untying the Knots

Thus far we have attempted to restructure your physical and psychological self, making you now an unraveled ball of twine, ready to be knitted into a brand-new wooly suit.

The question is, what style do you want it to be this time around?

"Oh geez ... there you go again. Three sentences of common sense, and now you're knitting some ridiculous wooly thing."

"What's the problem?"

"No one is going to buy that—they are adults, you know."

"Yes, I do know, and that is the problem, They have forgotten how to wonder ..."

"I don't understand."

"That's because in the work world, you were so occupied with raising a family, getting the next promotion, or meeting a deadline that you did not even notice that you were being trained not to question anything."

"Why do you say that?"

"In the world of work, most people agree to play nice and do what they are told in exchange for money. They keep their crazy, innovative ideas to themselves and hope that no one asks them a question to which they don't know the answer."

"And your point is?"

"Now that you are finally free to do whatever you want, you are also free to figure out how to return to the place where you enjoyed learning and you welcomed new experiences."

Looking Back, Living Forward

We fully expect that many people will view this section of the book with a fair amount of skepticism and possibly dismiss some of the ideas outright. This is understandable because many people are not raised to search within themselves for the answers to problems and personal growth, but this does not mean that the following ideas are any less valid.

Indeed, in many cultures around the world, the notion that you should endeavor to evolve yourself is not as high on the list of personal goals. Many cultures, or strata of society, actually work on the maxim that "this is your lot in life; get on with it." So perhaps in these later, freer years of your life, you can finally take a fresh look at what you want to be in life. You now have the freedom of choice to consider a variety of changes to your lifestyle.

For the purposes of discussion, we are going to omit references to religion, psychology, and strange things like chakras, and just talk about these changes themselves to help everyone consider the merit of the ideas without getting too hung up on labels. Those who come away from this book wanting more detailed information will find that they naturally will lead themselves to it, and if this does not happen, they can search for information relating to just about any topic in this book on the Internet. The online world has opened up such a diverse range of places to search, whether through search engines, surfing, or links provided by other people. There is virtually no subject untouched in today's online world. At the click of the mouse, you can read about yoga in Goa, then a few seconds later find out where the best yoga places are in California, and then find the cheapest air travel to get there. Perseverance, patience, and a degree of plausibility about what you are reading are all basic requirements of the self-learning process but well worth the time and effort.

To begin the discussion, let's start with a simple question: "Are you creating a loving, abundant, supportive life for yourself that excites you to get out of bed in the morning?"

If your answer is "Yes, isn't everyone?" you are in the wrong class.

If, however, you are just a little confused as to how your life slipped by to this point without your noticing, the question becomes not so much "*How* did I get here" as "*Where* do I need to go, *and what do I need to do?*"

Lots of people recommend spending a great deal of time analyzing the past instead of getting on with their journey, and that is fine for the young, who have the luxury of time on their side. But if you are like most Oldsters, you probably have more gray hair than time to waste, so let's be pragmatic and spend as little time as possible sloshing around in a murky past that we can't always recall clearly and can do little to change at this point anyway. After all, if you could turn the clocks back, would you really have done things that much differently?

HAPPINESS
IS NOT LOOKING BACK
YOU'RE NOT
GOING THAT WAY

Clearly, there are events, experiences, and learning curves that took place in your past that shaped you into who you are today. In certain cases, some of those past issues may be worth reconsideration or rethinking, now that you have more time and are more mature. Maybe there are things that could have been done better, which now, in later years, when you have the time and patience to revisit them, might be worthwhile. You won't climb Mount Everest again for sure, but the drive and enthusiasm that you possessed when you were younger may be the goal to strive for in your later years. Some call it "rediscovering the passion again." You may be able to rekindle the creativity you seemed to have years ago, which has been muted through external or societal pressure, built up over many years.

In his book *Situation Ethics: The New Morality*, Joseph Fletcher states that a person's action or reaction to any given situation depends on the situation *at the time*. In other words, he says that you do what comes naturally to you at the moment it happens. It may turn out to have been a poor choice, of course, and there may have been consequences, but the fact that you were in control of your decision and acted upon it is the critical issue. It is that control element that you are striving to retrieve in your Third Journey.

Of course, you planned for the changes in your life as much as the situation permitted, and you sought whatever guidance was available, but at the end of the day, you did whatever you decided you had to do to keep moving forward. We can look back on some of these situations with pride; some others not so much …

There is no point in wasting time looking back and saying, "If only …" It is fine to haul out the family album once in a while and remember happy times, but it does not do well to spend too much time doing this at the same point in your life when your children are grown and scattering to the four winds, building families of their own. Moreover, if your past relationships are full of baggage, best leave the boxes undisturbed in the cellar than go poking about, stirring up old pain, unless you believe that there are residual issues that are preventing you from moving forward. Unresolved matters such as these *should* be addressed, and it may be that you need to look backward to allow yourself to look forward. A thorough and successful analysis of the past may open up new doors in your life that you thought had been slammed shut.

The Power of Self-Belief

Now that you have left the past where it belongs, it is time to talk about what you are going to do to regenerate your sense of personal power. This concept confuses a lot of Oldsters in the beginning because popular wisdom is that once you retire, you should be happy giving up all the responsibility that you were burdened with in the work world. The reality is, however, that your Third Journey affords you the time and freedom to regain or solidify control of your life. For some people that newfound power can be enlightening; for some, it's too much pressure, but the fact remains that you now have the freedom to change your lifestyle, should you so choose. Clearly, family responsibilities or societal pressures will impact or influence your ability to change, but you have reached a stage in your life where your personal preferences can and should be uppermost.

Having said this, however, the stresses that used to occupy your thoughts need to be replaced with something more fulfilling that nurtures your self-esteem and excites your creativity so that you do not wind up feeling lackluster and powerless to change your circumstances.

In your Third Journey, you have the opportunity to become very finely balanced or to completely fall apart. Since most of us are not really cut out to be Jedi masters, let's strive to regenerate ourselves to a point somewhere in between.

Sounds simple, right?

If only it were.

The very concept of what it means to have a happy retirement is in transition. Although there is a continuing temptation to obsess about how little time is left, it is much more beneficial to focus *on how much you can still achieve and how you can draw upon your personal wisdom and talents to make a lasting contribution to the world.*

The challenge is that the older you get, the more you need enrichment to maintain your positivity and zest for life, but now that you have passed through the retirement threshold, you have a lot more free time to fill.[52] When you were in the work world, your employer or your family filled your day. Now everything is up to you, and you may find it challenging to provide sufficient stimulation for yourself if you have not planned a nice meaty project for you to sink your teeth into right away (or the one that you had in mind is not living up to your expectations).

So what is a newly freed spirit to do?

You can stick to your guns and decide not to change anything about your diet, your personal habits, or your vices (you know what we are talking about!), and let an insurance actuary attempt to predict how long you will be with us. Or you can decide to regenerate your desire to improve yourself, and find out just how much this new world you have landed in has to offer.

The challenge for the current crop of Oldsters is that the world is undergoing a transformation all its own in which we are migrating away from a traditional view of the aging process to a new social reality that is not yet completely evolved. A traditional upbringing would have you believe that once you reach the age of sixty-five, all you can do is grow old and pass away.

If you reject this notion, then you are going to have to reprogram your thinking. No one knows how much time he or she has left, so you might as well get out of bed every day and *live* a life of constructive defiance. So what if you are sixty-five or seventy-five or eighty-five? Who says you can't take up painting or photography or poetry or Chinese cooking or learn Swahili? Who says you can't take dance classes, or wear purple, or go on a date? It's your life. Go ahead and live it.

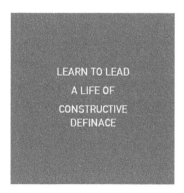

LEARN TO LEAD
A LIFE OF
CONSTRUCTIVE
DEFINACE

---

52. "Keep in mind that excess time on your hands is not so much a problem as it is a tremendous resource you haven't yet learned how to use."—Dr. Bob Ritzema.

For some Oldsters, being the world's best granny is bliss itself. Others need to do something more altruistic to make the world a better place. Still others build houses for Habitat for Humanity or write books. Still others might find it much more productive to spend a sunny afternoon staring at the clouds and wondering, "What new things can I do in my life now?"

Keep in mind that different temperaments need different types of stimulation, and now that you have had a taste of freedom you are unlikely to be satisfied by the same type of job that you used to do, even if you need the money. Going back to work rarely seems fulfilling unless you completely change your profession or possibly start your own company.

Building Your Self-Fulfillment

One of the easiest ways to maintain a sense of fulfillment is to work on your personal relationships with friends, family, and members of the community. If you have not been a social butterfly up to this point, now is the perfect time to go out and rejuvenate your social skills. This can seem a daunting task to someone who has been a loner (or, conversely, who has never been alone before), but change is good for the soul. Isolation, however, is not. Your self-confidence and social skills are just like your muscles—if you don't exercise them, they become weak. Left unchecked, it is possible to become so fearful of being emotionally wounded that you start sabotaging your relationships through mistrust and anger.

We appreciate that some people keep to themselves because they have been deeply wounded by others, and we are not going to attempt to push you to make changes in this area if you are at peace with your situation. In fact, there are many people who much prefer their own company to spending time with people they don't know (or don't like). They don't see solitude as a bad thing. They travel alone, they dine out alone, they watch sports alone, they go hill-climbing alone, and they much prefer to go shopping alone. The need for companionship is not a high priority for them.

If this is not you, however, and you really do wish that you knew how to break out of the cocoon of isolation you have built around yourself, simply decide that you are going to do one uncomfortable thing every day and have one uncomfortable conversation until it gets a little easier. This is not as bad as it sounds—librarians, hotel concierges, waitresses, hairdressers, and most store employees are paid to chat with the public. Feel free to practice on them as much as you like until you are ready to join some sort of a social club or gathering.

Strengthening your bonds with your fellow humans will also eventually help you to feel more of a connection to the universe itself. One of the most difficult things to come to terms with as we age is the question of whether there is a higher power and if there is continued existence beyond what we experience here on earth.

If you are reading this, and you are devoutly religious, please do not be offended by this suggestion. There are a great number of Oldsters who are not nearly as certain about what comes next (if anything). Research conducted at the University of Chicago seems to indicate that the "largest increases in belief in God most often occur among those 58 years of age and older. This suggests that belief in a higher power is especially likely to increase among the oldest groups, perhaps in response to the increasing anticipation of mortality."[53] While we are not about to debate the merits of any religion or system of beliefs, we do suggest that you make peace with your version of the truth. and spend your time focusing on the things that you still need to accomplish in this lifetime.[54] It does not do to spend the last third of your life worrying about dying. Not only does it defeat the purpose of living, but it is ultimately an unpreventable event.

---

53. International surveys conducted by NORC at the University of Chicago in 2012 to measure the depth of people's belief in God reveal vast differences among nations, ranging from 94 percent of people in the Philippines who said they always believed in God, compared to only 13 percent of people in the former East Germany.

54. We acknowledge that area of religious beliefs is quite complex, and while it may be an obstacle to growth for some, it may the path to growth for others. The point is to come to some sort of acceptance regarding your beliefs.

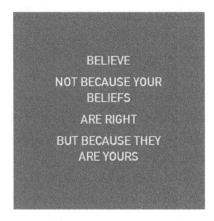

BELIEVE
NOT BECAUSE YOUR
BELIEFS
ARE RIGHT
BUT BECAUSE THEY
ARE YOURS

If you don't know what to think about the possibility of an existence beyond what we experience here on earth, consider the following:

If there is some sort of existence
Beyond what we experience here on earth,
Neither believing in it,
Nor not believing in it
Would change the fact of its existence.

What does matter is that we are here on earth now, and we have the ability and the opportunity to learn and grow *the entire time* that we are here. To squander this opportunity is to waste life itself. If you doubt this, just have a chat with anyone battling a serious illness, and you will discover one of two things: they are either filled with regret regarding all the things they did not do when they were healthy, or they are clawing their way out of bed every morning, determined to continue to live life to the fullest on their own terms, in defiance of their circumstances.

These people have a tremendous will to live and show us just how much can be accomplished. Steve Jobs, for example, the founder and CEO of Apple, lived and worked for seven years with a rare form of pancreatic cancer and actually made several of his largest contributions to the advancement of technology *after* his diagnosis. It is thought that the way Jobs handled his cancer will most certainly leave a lasting impact on others living with a potentially deadly disease.

The further you go in your Third Journey, the more your ability to support your desire to experience life becomes critical to your happiness (if not your very survival). Sometimes it is simply the strength of your desire to take the next step that determines your ability to do so.

If you do not self-regenerate or at least don't take the time to consider some form of regeneration, you run the risk that it will become more and more difficult to keep up with the fast-paced changes of modern life. Regeneration, especially self-regeneration, is a very personal issue—there is no "one size fits all." You should make every effort to analyze the lifestyle you have had thus far, consider making changes for the future, and above all else take full control of your lifestyle. Even if you are facing health challenges, never forget that no one really knows how much time they have, so don't be afraid to set some goals, make some plans, and have some fun living.

Top Ten Tips for Your Journey

1. Don't look back too often; you can't change the past.
2. Don't give in to your fears or concerns. Face and embrace them.
3. Don't ignore your passion. Get excited about new things.
4. Don't follow others. Chart your own course.
5. Don't look back and say, "If only." Look forward and say, "I will."
6. Don't rely on your old perceptions of retirement—refresh and restart.
7. Don't look back with regret. Look forward with joy.
8. Don't forget your past. It's what made you.
9. Don't let your circumstances prevent you from living each day to the fullest.
10. Think young, but act your age.

READY, STEADY, GO

Making Final Preparations for Your Journey

By the time it came to the edge of the Forest, the stream had
grown up, so that it was almost a river, and, being grown-up,
it did not run and jump and sparkle along as it used to do
when it was younger, but moved more slowly. For it knew
now where it was going, and it said to itself, "There is no
hurry. We shall get there some day." But all the little streams
higher up in the Forest went this way and that, quickly,
eagerly, having so much to find out before it was too late.
—A. A. Milne, *The House at Pooh Corner*

If you have meandered along through this book, you have wandered the
forest path with us and now have arrived at a sunny meadow filled with
wildflowers. There is a soft breeze and a well-placed rock on which to sit
and think for a bit. With any luck, you have reached some conclusions
regarding the areas of your life that are just as you would like them to
be, and you have identified a few things that you want to change before
proceeding with the journey of a lifetime.

Regardless of whether you are entering the postwork world for the
very first time or simply pausing to rest and regroup midway through
your trip, this is your time to exhale and reassure yourself that no matter

the challenges, the rest of your life can be so much more than you ever imagined.

Yes, you will still have responsibilities at home and bills to pay, but you are finally able to choose the life you want and do the things you like.

Reaching a New Self-Awareness

It is of little consequence that it has taken this length of time to reach an elevated state of self-awareness through growing up, working hard, raising a family, and coping with everything life has thrown at you. Those things are all behind you now. The things that once seemed so challenging have served their purpose, bringing happiness and sadness to your daily life. They have enabled you to figure out what you like and what you don't like, *and they have left you with the wisdom* to incorporate into your life as many of the things that you enjoy as possible, while still respecting their impact on others around you.

As we age, the need for self-fulfillment increases. Now that we are finally free from the obligations of work, it is perfectly reasonable to want to do things in our lives that we have yearned to do for many years. If you are on your own, providing you stay within your economic means, there is literally no need to justify your desires to anyone, especially yourself, because if you don't do these things now, when will you do them?

Moreover, if you are living with the person who has been at your side, it is not really feasible to leave him or her behind if that person is holding you back. You are going to have to find the middle ground, even if that is not easy.

So where does this leave you?

Finalizing Your Plan

Hopefully, you're sitting at the kitchen table, planning an adventure together or at least negotiating the terms of your new détente agreement. Obviously, we suggest that you at least try to find a few things that you and your partner can do together regularly and also agree to scheduled "me time," in which you will both happily go your separate ways and then meet up for supper. The point is to get out there and try things.

It is quite okay if some things turn out to be disappointing or maybe less than expected because the satisfaction level of at least having tried it will be significant. In many respects, the actual doing of something (e.g., traveling to see the pyramids) can often be less enjoyable than the planning and the excitement beforehand. "I'm really looking forward to doing [this or that]" becomes a self-fulfilling motivation to get off the couch and make the arrangements.

The trick to a long and successful Third Journey is to be honest with yourself and your life partner (if you have one) regarding what you like to do and how you want to spend your time. However, the challenge as you age is to learn to like whatever you are doing and appreciate the life that you have, over and over again, and not allow the loss of bygone days to overcome you. This is neither easier nor harder for those on their own or those accompanied by family members; it is simply different.

If our life partners have the same likes as we do, then harmony prevails. If one partner's likes are different from the other partner, however, then "live and let live" must become the mantra for both of you.

Life Is Not a Rehearsal

We all get one shot at it. If you constrain the wishes of your partner, you will both suffer. Your relationship will become a battle of wills regarding who gets to do what they want, rather than a partnership continually building a life from the things that you like to do together. You will have depressed, empty, silent days when you might have had comfort, companionship, and stimulation.

If your partner is determined to be selfish and ignore your needs and desires, you must make peace with the fact that while he or she is not living up to *your* expectations, he or she is also unconsciously giving you the freedom and permission to discover what *you* like and to go do it. Sitting home alone, angry that your partner is not there with you, is no way to live out your days. Equally, you have no right to attempt to make your partner feel guilty if he or she has figured out what he or she wants to do with his or her time, but you are not willing to participate in these activities, regardless of your reasons.

If you live alone, then you really only have one person to consult, and ironically, only one person to blame if you are not enjoying yourself! If you are letting sorrow, self-pity, and loneliness stop you from having happy experiences, face up to this, and find ways to make your days busier until you start to feel better or find people in worse shape than you are to help. There is nothing like realizing how lucky you are to chase the blues away.

Maintaining a Positive Attitude

A positive attitude and a desire to keep learning are the keys to a long and happy Third Journey. Information provides us with the opportunity to enjoy the most appropriate lifestyle for each of us to reach a level of peace, stability, and contentment in our latter years.

Being True to Yourself

In today's world of technology, we can easily research and make very personal decisions about what we like, about what we might like to try, and about what makes us happy. The old adage "To thine own self be true" has never been more poignant, for the further you go, the more critical it becomes to understand and embrace a life of doing what you like. On a superficial level, this is often dismissed as being selfish, but it's not. Doing what you want is selfish; doing what you like is liberating. Understanding the subtle yet sublime difference between the two is the essence of life. The Third Journey is the most critical journey of your life, now that you are in your sunset years. You can't live like a teenager anymore; you also can't live as a middle-aged, income-generating person ever again. You can only live today and plan for tomorrow.

Having the knowledge to determine your lifestyle is the undeniable facilitator of change. Let knowledge open your eyes, your mind, and your heart to experience the variety of choices that you really do have.

It is our hope that our Third Journey book has not only helped you find a way to begin anew today but that it also will provide an ongoing reference for you to revisit time and time again, as a source of inspiration, encouragement, and advice and to recharge your motivation and determination to enjoy the thrill of the Third Journey. This can be the most exciting stage of a person's life, and with the proper help and guidance, you can turn the third stage from a near-the-end feeling to a worthwhile and rewarding journey.

> "If you can dream it, you can do it."
> —Walt Disney

APPENDIX A

The Economy Will Go *Boom*

Prologue to Appendix A

This book, *The Third Journey*, was written at the individual level. It is intended to help people approaching or in retirement to navigate the many and, at times, complex issues that arise in the golden years.

Yet no book about the fastest-growing segment of the community (anywhere)—the so-called baby boomers—would be complete without at least a cursory look at the impact they have and will increasingly have on every facet of life and economies in their neighborhood, their city, and their country. The economic power of this generation is enormous and will heavily impact industries, social services, goods and services, governments, national budgets, and cultural lifestyles around the world. Change will occur.

So we have chosen to close *The Third Journey* with a peek into the future. Some predictions, some guesses, some dreams, but above all else, hopefully, we leave you to ponder the *fact* that we, the baby boomers, have a voice and a place in society. While the Third Journey is a very personal trip, don't forget that together we can change society and maybe the world.

Let's see where the Third Journey train might take us.

The Economic Power of the Olderhood Generation

In the United States, for example, some ten thousand people turn sixty-five every day—a figure that is accelerating; fifteen years ago, it was seven thousand per day. Even for a large, heavily populated country, that is a staggering number. And even though it is spread across large, vast areas of land, cities, and states, the cumulative impact and spending power of the boomers is having a dramatic effect on health and services, housing, spending patterns, economic growth, and financial markets.

If it can be agreed that the working population currently drives the economy, while the retired population is largely unproductive, in national economic terms (e.g., GDP), then the ever-increasing predominance of Oldsters will have serious repercussions in the years to come. In particular, the taxation revenues of national governments will be lowered, while the payouts on programs such as state pensions will increase, creating a deficit that must be recovered somewhere else.

Percentage of the population aged 65 and over:

Country	Year 2014	Year 2050
Japan	25.8%	40.1%
Germany	21.1%	30.1%
France	18.3%	25.8%
UK	17.5%	23.6%
Canada	17.3%	26.3%
U.S.	14.5%	20.9%

Source: US Census Bureau International Database

Life expectancy rates are climbing rapidly due to better health, better medical care, better financial status, and more information online to raise awareness of retirement issues sooner. The upswing is significant around the world, and life in 2050 will be very different for the inhabitants of this planet than it is today. Certain sectors of our communities (and their supporting social services) will be significantly affected.

Health Care

Health care in particular will be increasingly affected by the boomer effect. As medical technology advances, as it is currently doing and will continue to do so, at a rapid pace, then the demand for better medical solutions will increase. People will expect to get the most advanced medical attention, but if the number of medical professionals and technicians decreases, while the number of retired customers increases, the supply and demand factor will become critical. Unless the health care industry itself is revolutionized, there just won't be enough care workers to go around, regardless of whether health insurance can pay for them.

The end result could easily be that long waiting lists for retirees (and, for that matter, those still in the workforce) to receive health care may become the norm. If the current emerging trend continues in the developed world, the focus will migrate away from the public health care sector to the private sector, and those retirees who are less well off may find their health care seriously affected. Private health insurance will become one of the leading expenses in everyone's budget, retired or still working.

Travel and Leisure

Travel and recreational facilities will also be impacted. This boomer generation is the wealthiest retirement population the world has ever experienced. The demand for easy-access travel, due to increased disposable income, will increase—and the travel industry will have to move swiftly and with targeted attention to accommodate Oldsters.

For example, if the retiree prefers the cruise vacation over the air/land vacation, then more cruise ships will be required. If longer-distance travel (international, for example) is required, then the need for larger airplanes will increase. The destinations that provide the right mix of security, Oldster-focused activities, ease of access, and onsite medical services will be best positioned to corner the market. More hotel rooms in specific locations will be required—not necessarily more luxurious rooms, just more of them. The retiree population, while having more disposable income, are equally wise when it comes to spending (they don't know how long they will live, so rash spending may drain their resources too soon). The term *frugal travel* may become popular.

There will be more demand for recreational facilities, such as golf clubs, swimming pools, and quiet garden settings in public areas. Entertainment venues that offer senior discounts and daytime performances will see their attendance soar. Demand for more walk-in and low-cost educational programs at colleges or senior learning centers will increase. Learning will accelerate as a key pastime of the active Oldster.

Real Estate

Real estate will change. As Oldsters think about downsizing, the demand for small condo living will increase, while the large homes they vacate will drop in value. It doesn't matter if the actual percentage of Oldsters who decide to downsize doesn't change much (presently about 70 percent of Oldsters expect to die in their existing homes). The sheer volume of them will have a major economic impact across every country. House values will swing considerably.

The Money Business

Financial considerations will become critically important. In many countries, the issue of sustainability of the state pension and/or social insurance payments is of grave concern, due to shifting population patterns, but the realistic impact will be of much less concern. There is no responsible government on earth that would intentionally allow its state pension pot to run dry. The civil unrest would be immense. The cry for government budgets to be slashed across various sectors—for example, defense spending—would far exceed any electoral acceptance of reducing or eliminating Oldsters' pensions. It won't happen in jurisdictions where the electoral process functions freely, but some political parties may learn this the hard way.

Financial investment patterns will certainly change. The heretofore notion that Oldsters only want to invest in fixed-income, high-quality securities will diminish. As Oldsters realize that they may have twenty years or more to live, then their need for safe investments, while important, will slowly veer toward a slightly riskier income-generating portfolio— due to their reasonable belief that they *will* live longer and have time to recoup any losses, should they arise down the line. Therefore, pension managers, investment managers, and mutual fund managers will have to rethink their recommended investment strategy for postwork Oldsters. The conservative managers will find that their more adventurous competitors will gain traction—and they will have to adapt to keep up.

Life insurance products, which are typically geared toward a retirement age of sixty-five and actuarial assessments of mortality soon thereafter, will have to slide their projections to the right of the curve. People buying life insurance policies in their twenties will be looking for coverage for well over fifty years—a very long time to invest the premiums, and the due diligence of life insurance companies will come under intense scrutiny. Will the company be in existence twenty years from now, much less fifty?

Health insurance will change dramatically. Again, the sheer numbers of Oldsters demanding quality service will place immense strain on the health insurance industry. They will find it difficult, if not impossible, to keep premiums at manageable levels under the current health care structure. Consequently, if your premiums in retirement today are high, brace yourself. You should be careful to ensure you have enough income to cover increased insurance costs. It is not possible to predict how high the premiums will go of course, but there will be significant uptick. Large amounts of new capital will have to channeled to the insurance industry to protect the huge increases in demand.

Consumer Products

As we live longer and there are more of us, the retirement market will demand more products, just in terms of quantity. If a retiree in the 1960s needed one refrigerator between age sixty-five and his passing, the chances are that nowadays the retiree will need two. He will live longer, and the population numbers will be more. Hence, the refrigerator manufacturers will have to produce more of them. This trend will have traction across all forms of consumer products, and more. The consumer product companies (and many other sales organizations) will have to rethink and refocus their marketing.[55]

The idea that today's retirement consumers buy incontinence products and not much else is incredibly short-sighted. The young marketing expert will soon realize that speaking to a sixty-five-year-old today will be pointless if he adopts the over-the-hill sales pitch. The consumer is not too dumb to understand complicated products, not too frail to try new gadgets, not too stupid to try new technologies, and certainly not too cost-conscious to just buy the cheap rubbish. Advertising strategies will have to change.

The Food Industry

Food, diet, and exercise issues will become even more interesting to the retirement community. Living longer is one thing, but living better or healthier will become a lifelong fascination for Oldsters. If we think we might live longer than our parents and grandparents, yet realize that our ability to do so is dependent on our well-being, which is a critical component of that, then we will pay closer attention to what we eat, how much we eat, when we eat, what vitamins we consume, what beverages we take, and what the effect of alcohol is on our bodies. And we will begin to take an ever-increasing interest in some form of exercise, mild or otherwise.

So we will demand better information from producers, better quality of preparation of food, more awareness of calories, and so forth. We will demand better quality vitamins and energy drinks. We will look for senior-friendly gyms and exercise clubs (we may even rename the word "gym" to something more attractive and less daunting). Manufacturers of exercise equipment will begin to think about targeting the seniors and not the Spandex twenty-five-year-olds who show up at the gym to flex body parts to impress the opposite sex. We might even get equipment

---

55. Only about 15 percent of advertising dollars are spent on the retiree demographic, despite accounting for almost half of consumer packaged-goods sales, according to Nielsen data.

we can use, given our weaker (let's be kinder and say *less strong*) bodies. Senior discounts will become the standard in gyms. If they aren't, we won't go to their gym. Simple as that.

Spending Power

Spending power is one of those interesting statistics that really doesn't mean that much in the grand scheme of things. While we recognize that the spending power of Oldsters is immense—in 2017, approaching *half* of the US adult population will be fifty and older, and they will control a full 70 percent of the disposable income, according to data tracker Nielsen[56]— the reality is that unless we band together and go to a big-box store on the same day to buy the same stuff (so they can see the true value of our spending power in one glorious day of sales), our power is currently very fragmented.

Nonetheless, as the older demographic increases in both numbers and wealth, and our health is good, and our lifestyle interests expand, we will consequently buy more of lots of things—consumer products or financial products or services such as travel and leisure—in total nationwide. In total spending terms, today's retiree market will be the predominant spending demographic. We will learn; we will explore; we will try new things; we will still buy fashion; we will still buy personal care products and vitamins, prescription drugs, new cars, face creams, and so forth.

As we discussed earlier in this book, Oldsters are frugal-minded. We are more in tune with our finances and our spending patterns, and we do know how to spend wisely. We won't spend money stupidly. Yet more than any other retirement generation, we are prepared to consider spending on things to excite us and to improve our overall lifestyle. We want to enjoy ourselves, and we'll spend accordingly. Therefore, our impact on the overall economy is staggering today but will increase exponentially. As a group, our spending capacity is enormous, so while it may not translate into power, per se, it is without question the largest

---

56. *The Me Generation Meets Generation Me*, Nielsen Report, last modified June 20, 2013, http://www.nielsen.com/us/en/insights/news/2013/the-me-generation-meets-generation-me.html.

percentage of any and all other groups on the planet. And will increase, year after year.

The old adage of *caveat emptor* ("let the buyer beware") is changing radically to "caveat seller"—let the seller take notice that we, as Oldsters, are here, both in numbers and in money, and to ignore us would be ill advised and, quite frankly, rather silly.

So as we wait for the corporate world to invent, or create, or design, and then produce goods and services for us, we'll just be getting on with our lives anyway, thank you very much.

Maybe we don't fully understand what we want. Maybe we'll just have to get on with whatever it is we think we like. Maybe we'll never know. But then again, maybe it doesn't matter.

In the meantime, let's just seek happiness and peace of mind … and when we find it, embrace it.

Top Ten Tips for Your Journey—Hop Aboard

1. It's time to let the economy work for you.
2. Keep in mind that you are part of the fastest-growing group in society.
3. Keep abreast of health care developments, advances, and costs.
4. Watch for travel deals; you can travel any time to take advantage.
5. If you are contemplating downsizing, be very cautious about price trends.
6. Keep track of all your pensions at least annually.
7. Watch out for goods and services sales; you have no rush to buy.
8. Be aware of quality food, and, if affordable, buy the good stuff.
9. Shop around for everything from coffee to couches.
10. Never be scared to ask for a discount. Remember—you are frugal.

APPENDIX B

Forming a Local Chapter of the Olderhood International Club

The Olderhood International Club (OIC) thrives on friendship and freedom of expression. You are encouraged to start your own local club as a means to enable Oldsters to gather together in whatever manner suits you best. You don't have to have a specified number of members, and you don't have to meet in a particular place or conduct formal meetings. You are free to be any sort of group that meets anywhere peaceful gatherings are permitted in your country.

While it is the intention of the OIC that members be at least fifty years of age, common sense should prevail, and volunteers who transport members to outings should be welcome to participate.

Please note that the OIC is *not* a dating club and does not subscribe to any political or religious affiliations or doctrines whatsoever. Please respect this one guideline at all times.

What to Do to Get Started

- *Register your chapter* by sending an e-mail to wrsl@ibl.bm, and provide your chapter name, location, e-mail address, and Skype address (if you have one). Chapter founders will be invited to participate in monthly webcasts and will be responsible for collecting annual chapter membership dues (suggested annual donation is ten dollars per person).

- Start a Facebook page for your chapter so that your members can chat online in a safe environment and find out about upcoming events.
- Hold a chapter meeting and post fun photos of your activities online.
- *Recruit additional members by posting invitations to join on the main Olderhood Facebook page.*

GLOSSARY FOR YOUR THIRD JOURNEY

annuity	A form of insurance or investment entitling the investor to a series of fixed annual sums, typically for the rest of his or her life. An annuity is most often paid to a retired person but can be paid to a person of any age.
baby boomer	A person born between 1946 and 1964, the oldest of whom started to reach traditional retirement age in 2012. Baby boomers are the first generation to pass through the retirement threshold in large numbers with sufficient health, wealth, energy, and technology to make the Third Journey as a collective.
bathroom pharmacy	The proliferation of over-the-counter pills, potions, and lotions that people self-administer at home instead of listening to what their bodies are trying to tell them or consulting a medical professional for a diagnosis and course of treatment.
bucket list	A wish list of the experiences and achievements that a person hopes to have or accomplish during his or her lifetime. Retirees in particular often have a list of things to do, places to visit, people to meet, and so forth. The term comes from doing something before the person "kicks the bucket."

budget	An overview of all sources of income and expenditure for a set period of time into a combined statement of finance (perhaps in a spreadsheet format). The budget should be reviewed at least annually and adjustments made to lifestyle, if appropriate.
chronic inflammation	Inflammation is actually an essential function of the healing process because it is your body's lifesaving response to the presence of disease-causing bacteria, viruses, and parasites. Under normal circumstances, when a pathogen enters the body, inflammation quickly surrounds and subdues both invader and any infected tissue and then subsides so that the healing process can begin. When the inflammation does not subside as it should, a chronic condition can develop.
deficit	The shortfall at the end of every month/year after all income has been received and all expenses made. This is a serious situation to be in and cannot be sustained for any length of time, unless you intend to fill the void through the sale of assets, such as your house, investment portfolio, and so on.
disillusionment phase	The moment that an Oldster, now in retirement, first realizes that sustaining happiness in retirement requires continually adapting to change and future planning.
doer	The part of you that hums when you are doing something you enjoy. It requires mental and physical stimulation but does not always welcome change. Care must be taken to learn to enjoy the aging process itself in order to have a long, productive postwork life.

downsizing	Usually relates to selling your existing (large) house and buying a smaller, more manageable property to live in for the rest of your life. While financial issues are the most important part of this discussion, the emotional and logistical parts are of equal if not more importance.
drawdown pension scheme	A pension scheme that allows you to draw a certain predetermined amount as monthly pension, thus reducing the principal amount—counterbalanced by investment income/increase in value. The drawdown amount will be renegotiated annually, as opposed to the fixed pension amount under an annuity.
elder	A person who is by age deemed to be in the latter years of his or her life. Usually correlated with that person's being deemed to be wiser and more mature.
estate	The money, property, and assets of a person that can be passed on to individuals (usually family members) upon that person's death.
euphoria phase	The initial happiness, when in retirement, derived from simply being free from work.
fear of change	A turn of events in a person's life that creates a sense of fear, concern, or anxiety, caused by a change of circumstances, either self-created or caused by external events or decisions.
financial planning	A state of awareness of your income, expenses, assets, and liabilities, and configuring them into a cohesive and understandable plan that will serve as the financial base for your retirement lifestyle, both today and for the rest of your life.
food enabler	A person who supports or encourages another's bad eating habits by providing the person with inappropriate quantities or types of food.

WILLIAM R. STORIE AND ROBIN W. TRIMINGHAM

food intervention	Identifying and improving an unhealthy diet by providing advice, information, and access to better-quality nutritious food, tailored to the needs of a specific person.
free-fall phase	The point during your first year in the postwork world when you realize that life is spiraling out of control in unanticipated ways, and everything seems to cost twice as much as you thought it would.
freedom of choice	In these latter years of your life, the decisions you make about lifestyle should be entirely your own. While others may have an opinion or preference about aspects of your life, the final choice must always be yours.
fulfillment phase	The planned implementation of a personal vision.
future world	A term used to describe the type of lifestyle you would like to strive for in retirement. It should be based on a realistic plan with defined objectives and goals, rather than pie-in-the-sky dreams, and should be a personal vision.
hard impact	A term used to describe the real impact in tangible, visible terms of an event in a person's life, often a negative experience. A financial crash causes the tangible effect of less money and causes immediate and strongly felt distress.
immortality	No one lives forever; the fear of death is one of the deepest emotions in everyone. As we age, however, there is a quiet transition to the acceptance of inevitability, and in many respects the fear tends to become less, as it is replaced by a more mature desire to do as much as possible in the time available.

income-driven financial strategy	An investment approach that focuses on income generation through cash dividends and such, and not value change.
inheritance	The money, property, and assets that can be conveyed to a person (usually by an older relative) under the terms of a will.
initial mission	The purpose that you assigned yourself to fulfill in the work world. Initial missions are usually family- or work-oriented, although they can occasionally be philanthropic.
long-term relationship	A relationship typically between two or more people of the opposite or same sex, which has lasted for a significant number of years. The relationship can be within a marriage or with family or with friends.
longevity lottery	The idea that, all things being equal, everyone has the potential to live beyond the age of one hundred years, but the chances of our managing to reach this age are largely governed by circumstances that we are not really able to control, such as the onset of a terminal illness.
lump sum pension	The full or partial amount you are allowed to take from your pension fund in one single payment or withdrawal.
monetary depression	A term used to describe the psychological anxiety and stress associated with a lack of money, especially when there are no realistic ways to obtain more money during retirement.

Now Generation	Life after retirement is not in a holding pattern—it is the time to refresh your thinking, your ideas, your plans, and your lifestyle, and work to fulfill your true purpose now. People who believe that life should be lived in the "now" and not be focused on the past or on what may happen in the future.
Olderhood	A new, evolving phase of life beyond adulthood. We began in childhood, then we moved into adulthood. Now, as the years have moved along, we transition into Olderhood. Advances in health care, nutrition, and access to quality information are creating an expanding social demographic of energetic, independent, mature contributors to society—a generation that has much to give and much more it wants to learn. This phase of life is the period when these Oldsters realize that the word "now" has a meaning they have never thought much about before—the Now Generation.
Oldster	A vital, active, thriving person over the age of fifty who lives life to the fullest.
part-time employment	After formal retirement, the retiree may choose to continue productive activity in a part-time job for compensation. The part-time job may be in the same field as the earlier career or something very different. The job will typically take up between fifteen and twenty-five hours per week.
pension	A payment made to a person (annually or monthly) who has retired from the work world, from various sources built up throughout his or her working life. Company pension plans or state pension plans are the primary examples. The pension payments should be in place for the rest of your life.

preretirement financial planning	Finding out in advance, while you are still in an income-generating employment, what your income and expenses will be once you retire, both in the immediate postretirement phase and for the rest of your life, and making a strategic plan in accordance with what your monthly budget will be.
postretirement financial management	Assessing the impact of your income and expenses now that you are in retirement, and projected numbers have become real numbers. Determining if adjustments need to be made to either the calculations or your lifestyle.
postwork world	The lifestyle chosen by those who have now left the work world and have entered the retirement phase of their lives.
psychomotivation	An all-embracing phrase to convey the notion that what we do is largely, if not totally, controlled by how we feel about doing it and whether we can be motivated or inspired to do something of importance with, or in, our lives.
recovery phase	The true beginning of your Third Journey, in which you put aside the aspects of your old life that were spiraling out of control and make decisions regarding how you want the rest of your journey to be.
relevant lifestyle	Your lifestyle, including physical activities, must be in tune with your health, physicality, and financial and spiritual abilities. All your thoughts and decisions must be cognizant of your situation.
repurpose yourself	The act of coming up with a new job, purpose, or mission for yourself that you will energetically pursue during your Third Journey.

retiree	A person who has retired from the traditional workforce.
retirement happiness	A state of contentment and peace of mind that arises as the by-product of undertaking an active, vital Third Journey with purpose.
retirement threshold	The moment that you cease to be part of the work world and enter into the third phase of your life. This can occur through early retirement or mandatory retirement at age sixty-five or delayed retirement after sixty-five.
Sandwich Generation	A generation of people who care for their aging parents while supporting their own children simultaneously. This support can be financial, physical, or emotional.
second childhood	A situation in which an adult starts to behave like a child again, either for fun, out of selfishness, or as a result of diminished mental capacity.
senior	A traditional term implying that a person is retired or has reached "old age."
soft impact	Arising out of the same event as mentioned in hard impact, only this is the emotional or psychological effect of the event. Inability to sleep is an example, as a result of a financial crash and a reduction in available money to buy everyday groceries.
surplus	An amount of money left over at the end of each month/year after all income has been received and all expenses have been made. This surplus can be used for special expenses or placed into savings.
third phase of life	A time to challenge traditional boundaries and conquer old fears, while staying positive and finding a meaningful purpose to carry you through the rest of your life.

true purpose	Identifying and adopting a reason for being that you passionately pursue.
unexpected expense	Typically, the expenses you incur in retirement are relatively stable and fairly predictable. However, from time to time, a completely unexpected expense can arise for a variety of reasons. Depending on the severity of this expense, it may cause your financial projections to be thrown off and other major adjustments to your lifestyle to be made.
value-driven financial strategy	An investment approach that focuses substantially but not necessarily exclusively on increasing the value (principal) of the investment portfolio, and largely ignores the dividend or interest income there from.
will	A legally binding document, typically drafted by a legal professional, which expresses the desires and instructions of the retiree when he passes as to what action needs to be taken to dispose of his estate.
work purpose	The daily tasks of being employed.
work world	A generic term to describe where the employed person spends his or her working days.

Open Book Editions
A Berrett-Koehler Partner

Open Book Editions is a joint venture between Berrett-Koehler Publishers and Author Solutions, the market leader in self-publishing. There are many more aspiring authors who share Berrett-Koehler's mission than we can sustainably publish. To serve these authors, Open Book Editions offers a comprehensive self-publishing opportunity.

A Shared Mission

Open Book Editions welcomes authors who share the Berrett-Koehler mission— Creating a World That Works for All. We believe that to truly create a better world, action is needed at all levels—individual, organizational, and societal. At the individual level, our publications help people align their lives with their values and with their aspirations for a better world. At the organizational level, we promote progressive leadership and management practices, socially responsible approaches to business, and humane and effective organizations. At the societal level, we publish content that advances social and economic justice, shared prosperity, sustainability, and new solutions to national and global issues.

Open Book Editions represents a new way to further the BK mission and expand our community. We look forward to helping more authors challenge conventional thinking, introduce new ideas, and foster positive change.

For more information, see the Open Book Editions website:
http://www.iuniverse.com/Packages/OpenBookEditions.aspx

Join the BK Community! See exclusive author videos, join discussion groups, find out about upcoming events, read author blogs, and much more! http://bkcommunity.com/

CPSIA information can be obtained
at www.ICGtesting.com
Printed in the USA
LVHW04s2034020718
582503LV00003B/647/P